D0106816

got MILF?

The Modern Mom's
Guide to
Feeling Fabulous,
Looking Great,
and Rocking a Minivan

sarah maizes

BERKLEY BOOKS, NEW

THE BERKLEY PUBLISHING GROUP
Published by the Penguin Group
Penguin Group (USA) Inc.
375 Hudson Street, New York, New York 10014, USA
Penguin Group (Canada), 90 Eglinton Avenue East, Suite 700, Toronto, Ontario M4P 2Y3, Canada
(a division of Pearson Penguin Canada Inc.)
Penguin Books Ltd., 80 Strand, London WC2R 0RL, England
Penguin Group Ireland, 25 St. Stephen's Green, Dublin 2, Ireland (a division of Penguin Books Ltd.)
Penguin Group (Australia), 250 Camberwell Road, Camberwell, Victoria 3124, Australia
(a division of Pearson Australia Group Pty. Ltd.)
Penguin Books India Pvt. Ltd., 11 Community Centre, Panchsheel Park, New Delhi—110 017, India
Penguin Group (NZ), 67 Apollo Drive, Rosedale, North Shore 0632, New Zealand
(a division of Pearson New Zealand Ltd.)
Penguin Books (South Africa) (Pty.) Ltd., 24 Sturdee Avenue, Rosebank, Johannesburg 2196,
South Africa

Penguin Books Ltd., Registered Offices: 80 Strand, London WC2R 0RL, England

This is an original publication of The Berkley Publishing Group.

The publisher does not have any control over and does not assume any responsibility for author or
third-party websites or their content.

Copyright © 2011 by Sarah Maizes.
Illustrations © by Mari Renwick.
Cover art and design by Diana Kolsky.
Text design by Kristin del Rosario.

PRINTING HISTORY
Berkley trade paperback edition / April 2011

Library of Congress Cataloging-in-Publication Data

Maizes, Sarah.
  Got MILF? : the modern mom's guide to feeling fabulous, looking great, and rocking a
minivan / Sarah Maizes.
      p.   cm.
  Includes bibliographical references.
  ISBN 978-0-425-23904-9
  1. Mothers—Psychology.   ...erhood—Psychological aspects.   3. Body image in women.
I. Title.
  HQ759.M323 2011
  646.70085'2—dc22

                                                                                      2010051261

PRINTED IN THE UNITED STATES OF AMERICA

10   9   8   7   6   5   4   3   2   1

For Isabel, Olivia and Benjamin—
who made me a mom . . .

For Scott—
who made me a MILF

acknowledgments

I have so many people to thank for helping me write this book—help that came in so many forms: help writing the book, help selling the book, help editing the book. Help came in the form of playdates so I could write and finish edits, late-night e-mails containing completed questionnaires about schedules and sex habits (the two were not necessarily mutually exclusive . . .), and laughs, snickers and muffled giggles when presented with pieces of the book in draft form (my favorite type of help!).

First, I want to thank Scott Burn, my boyfriend (and the best friend I have EVER had), for asking me every day, "How's the book coming?" and my kids, Izzy, Livi and Ben, for "giving me something to write about" (their words . . . and my mom's) and for fixing their own snacks when I was writing.

I have to thank my Official MILF Board for sharing their wisdom with a candor only true MILFs could muster: Ilene Grossman, Debbie Farfel, Risa Kazdan, Laurey Levy, Wendy Marcus, Sharon Scott, Christina Simon, Tina Fuller Pomerance, Jodi Galen, Azy Farahmand, Danielle Swartz, Wendy Globerman, Robin Davids, Camille Hunter, Stephanie Millstone, Apryl Krakovsky, Elizabeth Ford, Robin Maizes and my big sister and role model for all things MILFy (and otherwise), Alison Dinerstein.

Of course, I also have to thank my MILF "pundits"— Michael Maizes, Stan Moger, Teo Hunter, Joey Plager, Michael Paraskevas, Tony Rago, Bob Bendick and the many other adorable men I forced to share their feelings.

I want to thank my ex-husband, Steven Maizes, for giving me three beautiful (and unwittingly hilarious) children; my "wife" and nanny, Cecelia Ixcot, for taking care of the kids when I couldn't do it all; Mari Renwick for her amazing artistic talents; and the gorgeous blond mom who sat next to me at the hair salon and used the phrase "maximum f@#kability."

I also have to thank my mom, Margery Schab, for teaching me the importance of a sense of humor and for supporting my writing even though the job doesn't come with health insurance.

And I want to give a HUGE thank-you (and a MASSIVE kiss and hug) to my beautifully fashionable, intelligent and MILFy agent, Elisabeth Weed, for "getting" me.

Her guidance, support and enthusiasm has released a genie that just won't go back in the bottle. And my beautiful, talented and incredibly tactful editor, Andie Avila, whose passion for all things MILFy (and belief that there is a MILF in all of us even before we have kids) made this book a reality.

contents

introduction

The other day a young male friend called me a MILF.

"Thanks?" was all I could think to say since I wasn't entirely sure if I had been insulted or not. His tone was complimentary, but a "MILF"? Really? I felt a little dirty. Maybe I'd heard him wrong. Maybe he needed a glass of "milk." Yes . . . that was it. After all, he was still in his twenties. Practically a growing boy . . . Let's see what's in the fridge. . . .

"You don't know what a MILF is, do you?"

Nope. He wasn't asking for milk. "Yes, I know what a MILF is." It wasn't a total lie. I had a *general* idea. . . .

"It's a 'Mother I'd Like to F@#k.'"

"DUH!!!" I knew I sounded like a high school girl, but he had caught me by surprise. I wasn't exactly sure what he was implying. If he thought I was going to have sex with him, he was very, very wrong. . . . That would change everything! After all, he was just a friend, and I had a boyfriend. Besides, he was really too young for me and . . .

He quickly backtracked. "I'm not saying *I* want to f@#k you; I'm just saying you're a MILF."

Whew! "Well, that's better," I said, pleased that crisis had been averted. (Okay, my ego quietly quipped, *What the hell do you mean you don't want to f@#k me?? This forty-year-old baby-makin' machine! You should be so lucky, you cocky little schmuck.* . . . Hey, I'm only human.)

Putting my ego aside, I tried to move on. I wasn't sure how a MILF would get past this awkward moment, so I did what came naturally. I offered him a slice of homemade chocolate cake and changed the topic of conversation. "So . . . about those Jets . . ."

Long after my friend left, his remark boinged around my skull like one of those Hi-Bounce rubber balls my son loves. I had been completely caught off guard by him calling me a MILF, and the fact he'd had to spell it out for me—and that "DUH!" had been my snappy comeback—didn't exactly fill me with pride.

I'm hip. (Stop laughing. . . .) I know a thing or two. I've been around the block. And even if I haven't been around a *particular* block, I at least like to give the impression that I have—that I know all the side streets and shortcuts. But I was completely unfamiliar with this neighborhood. It was like some exclusive gated community about which you always hear wild, sordid tales, but have never actually visited.

Of course I'd heard the term "MILF" before, usually in connection with porn, but I had never been referred to as one. I knew enough to know the word referred to a mom who was really "hot"—but I imagined someone who washed her car wearing jean shorts, like in the "Stacy's Mom" music video. I don't even own jean shorts. And if I did, I certainly wouldn't wash my car in them.

What exactly had he been thinking when he'd called me a MILF? What sparked the comment? Did he think I slept around? Had he seen my thong sticking out of my pants? (I pride myself on being a vigilant thong tucker. . . .) Maybe he just thought I was sexy. I mean, a guy could call a woman a MILF without having an agenda, right? . . . RIGHT?!

I wanted to know more about MILFs. Was calling someone a MILF rude or flattering? Had the term taken on new "street" meaning—like "bad" or "fly"? Was there some kind of MILF movement going on? And if I was indeed a MILF, were there more of us? Where would I find them? Was there a MILF union of some sort I could join, and if so, did they have dental?

I was determined to find out what exactly made a woman a MILF. Was a MILF a slut or a siren? More important, if someone called me a MILF and I simply smiled and said, "Thank you," was I inviting him to put his hand on my boob?

I was in virgin territory (which, needless to say, as a mother of three, I hadn't been in for a long time).

So I decided to research the topic thoroughly. I Googled "MILF." After scrolling through numerous porn sites' listings and learning a bit about the Moro Islamic Liberation Front, I found a definition on Wikipedia.org that seemed fairly inoffensive:

> **MILF** • *(slang)* Mother/Mom I'd Like to F@#k:
> A (putative) mother or woman of childbearing age
> found to be sexually attractive.

Well, that's not so bad. But sexually attractive? To him? I thought about the times my young male friend and I had spent together writing sketch comedy, performing improv and talking about life. I had never given him any impression that I was interested or available to him for sex. Besides, I was a divorced single mother with three kids under the age of eight. (Who doesn't want a piece of that?) I was pondering this further when one of my twins shook me out of my stupor by running into a doorjamb.

I went to assess the damage.

As I sat on the floor holding a pig-shaped ice pack to the forehead of my child, it dawned on me that I had in fact been paid a *huge* compliment! This great, funny guy, who was at least ten years my junior, was saying that he saw *me*, a divorced, over-thirty-five mom with three kids, as a *viable* sexual candidate—albeit not for him, but for *some* guy out there. It was safe to say that whatever he found "attractive" about me was definitely *not* based solely on looks. It couldn't possibly be. My midsection had experienced two pregnancies (one being a twin pregnancy), my graying roots needed vigilant attention and gravity was obviously stalking my ass (and was closing in fast). On top of that, as a busy mom of three, "primping" was now defined as showering for seven minutes rather than three, possibly using a hair dryer, and throwing on clothes I knew I didn't first have to smell. But this guy had met all three of my children, seen me bandage boo-boos, watched me wrangle them at the dinner table and heard me shriek, "GET IN THE TUB NOW!" till my pulsating vocal cords were visible through my open mouth. And he *still* thought I was pretty. Awww.

That was when I realized that being a MILF meant so much more than being "f@#kable." It meant that even though I was ready for a nap every day by eleven a.m., and my priorities had shifted from looking good to not smelling *too* bad, and instead of accenting my "charms" with pleasing, buttery-soft leather accoutrements, the "accessories" I now proudly toted talked back and needed help wiping—I was attractive. Nay, not just attractive, but sexy. And get this—being a mom didn't hinder my sexiness; it was part of what *made* me sexy!

This was hard to fathom. Apparently, that funny, exciting and vibrant woman I thought I had kissed farewell to in the lobby of Cedars-Sinai as they wheeled me up to labor was still hanging around. I hadn't lost myself just because I was a mom!

Being a MILF meant that the girl who laughed easily, who loved to travel, who believed in finding your passion and pursuing it was still alive! Frankly, there were times I thought she'd gone down with the ship once the tidal wave of motherhood swept over the bow. But there she was, in her little life raft, waving a tiny flag. What a trouper! I suddenly noticed her for the first time in years. I couldn't believe I hadn't seen it before. She'd been there all along. She was the one who organized movie nights with girlfriends, who took writing classes, who attempted a career in comedy and taught her children the importance of being beautiful on the inside. And you know what? She wasn't rail thin anymore, but she looked pretty darn good in her swimsuit frolicking with her kids and the dolphins in Mexico. Yep, she was cute, all right.

It was obvious being called a MILF was a compliment. In fact, it was the biggest compliment of all. It meant embracing motherhood and sexuality simultaneously. The concept was evolutionary!

I could own this. I deserved this! I would embrace being a MILF! Intrigued and thrilled by my newly discovered MILF-dom, I couldn't help but try it out. Like it was a shiny new car hot off the lot, I wanted to take it for a test-drive around the neighborhood. My first stop? Starbucks. Why? Because MILFy or not, without my caffeine for fuel, this mom wasn't going to make it around the block. I walked into Starbucks, head up, shoulders back and just plain feelin' good. I sidled up to the barista, looked him straight in the eye, smiled and said, "A venti vanilla latte . . . *please*." How often had I growled "venti vanilla latte" at this poor kid, whose misfortune it had been to encounter me every morning before I'd had my caffeine? He seemed surprised and pleased by this change in me, and with a big smile he gave me an extra dollop of foam and said, "Have a great day."

Wow! A little MILFiness could go a long way! There was no longer any doubt in my mind . . . I was onto something big.

And I continued on my way. I charmed the information guy at Barnes & Noble, and he gave me someone's saved copy of *Three Cups of Tea*. I winked spontaneously at my boyfriend, he was intrigued . . . and confused . . . but more intrigued. Feeling bolder and more confident, I wore more fabulous accessories; I took risks with my writing; I led my kids on interesting culinary expeditions in our kitchen and we all positively glowed from the shared experience. I stood taller; I felt happier; my family and I flourished. Being a MILF was great!

I suddenly saw MILFs everywhere. At the park, at the movies, at the market, at Gymboree. Beautiful women, HOT women, many with their kids in tow, and I noticed all the men (and women) checking them out. They wore everything from cardigans to sweats, jeans to business suits. Some pushed newborns in carriages, and others walked astride their texting teenagers. Some were models of fitness; others were new moms—swollen breasts straining against their James Perse cotton tees. But I noticed they all had one thing in common: they weren't "hot" despite their children—they were "hot" because of them. Their roles as moms thrust into sharp relief their confidence, pride and age-defying beauty. Their strong senses of self made them more complicated, more captivating and infinitely more intriguing creatures. There was just *more* to these women. They couldn't just walk, talk and chew gum at the same time—they could feed toddlers, buy groceries and organize a school fund-raiser armed with only a PDA, a broken crayon and some macaroni. Now, that's multitasking! These were women with families, responsibilities *and* passion. They didn't disappear behind their families—they stood out. They were sharp, savvy women who commanded you to take notice even as they were occupied with their offspring. These were whole women. Not girls. And they looked *really* f@#king great!

Being a MILF was a badge of honor!

I had unearthed a secret. A BIG secret. I had discovered that EVERY mom has the potential for MILFdom. You just need to take out your binoculars, scan the horizon of that swirling, churning ocean called "motherhood" and look for that chic little woman bobbing about in a dinghy and waving a flag! (I bet she keeps it in a really cute tote.)

And get this—maybe you know it already, or maybe what

I'm about to tell you will shock you—someone out there thinks you're hot. Really hot. Not your spouse, partner, boyfriend or that guy you have a restraining order against . . . No, someone else. Maybe someone at the market, at the movies, at a restaurant; maybe someone you were stuck next to in traffic. He saw you when you were completely unaware, watched you sing in your car, laugh at something funny or take a bite of something really, really delicious, and he thought, That's *a MILF*. And believe me, it's happened more than once.

No, no . . . don't go shower. Just because someone considers you a MILF, you should not feel "icky." It doesn't mean someone is undressing you with his eyes, fantasizing about you or memorizing your license plate number. Like Heath Ledger as the Joker said in *The Dark Knight*, "I'm a dog chasing cars. I wouldn't know what to do with one if I caught it." For men, it's the same thing. They enjoy the view—from afar. They noticed you and had a complimentary thought. But seriously, if they caught you? They wouldn't know what to do with you. You're too much for them. You're too much for most. You're an incredible, beautiful, fascinating woman, and being near you is exciting and pleasurable—it doesn't mean they want to chew on your bumper.

It's time to recognize the fact that you are MILF Material. Your spouse knows it; your girlfriends know it; even the girl who makes your caramel macchiato knows it—and she secretly wants to be just like you when she has kids. . . .

Now YOU need to own it and share your fabulousness with everyone around you! The time has come for MILFs everywhere to stand up and be counted!

We are not mothers who will gladly fade into the woodwork of our families and hide behind their achievements. We will not put aside our own wants and needs to make room for only the wants and needs of others. We will not set the example for our sons and daughters that choosing to have a family means choosing to lose ourselves. We will nurture our children, we will nurture ourselves and we will all thrive!

Say it with me. . . . "I am f@#kable! I am MILF! Hear *me* roar!"

what is a
MILF?

Got MILF?!

—ARI ON *ENTOURAGE* (HBO)
(CALLED OUT WHILE PASSING AN OLDER WOMAN JOGGING)

"What exactly is a MILF?" you ask. Is it a "Mother I'd Like to Have *Fun* With"? "A Mother I'd Like to Be *Friends* With"? Let me clarify.

While those two definitions apply (MILFs are both great friends and a HECK of a lot of fun), a "MILF" is what is technically known in popular culture as a "**M**other **I**'d **L**ike to **F**@#k." Now, let me save you some trouble and say what so many of you are already thinking: "EEEeeewwww, that's so gross!" "That's so disgusting!" "How degrading to women!" Yeah, yeah . . . Got that out of your system?

The origins of the word are crass. There's no getting around it. But over the past decade the term has morphed, evolved and been embraced by popular culture to create the more palatable and complimentary term to which we can now respond positively and even endearingly, much as we would if a friend called us "bee-yotch" or told us we were "phat."

The acronym, though impossible to date specifically, entered society in the 1970s. The term gained more rapid recognition in the nineties with the rise of the Internet (where pop culture thrives . . . as does porn), but MILF pundits agree that the expression was officially introduced into "proper" pop culture by the movie *American Pie* in 1999.

As teenagers, we all knew someone whose mom was "hot," and was referred to as such by the teenage boys who hung around and played Atari on the corduroy sofa. Beyond being gorgeous and vital and breathing new life into a plain white T-shirt, this was the same mom who made the best brownies on the block, kept Pop-Tarts in the cupboard and let the kids congregate in her basement (while keeping any improper "activities" in check). She was hip, she was cool, she was vibrant, but she never believed she was, wanted to be, or tried to be one of the gang. There's nothing MILFy about a woman clinging to her youth and hanging around a bunch of kids trying to be the center of attention. We've seen these moms. They hold themselves up as MILFs, but let me make this clear—they are *not* MILFs.

A MILF doesn't need to be the center of attention to feel beautiful. She has her own life, her own activites, better things to do—even if it's reading a good book. MILFs are independent, confident and self-possessed. And they give their kids the room to be the same. MILFs nurture but do not hinder. They engage but do not encroach. They facilitate but don't impose. It's this combination of coolness and self-sufficiency that makes a MILF so darn super hot. And although no one may have thought to call her a MILF back then, a MILF she was.

Today a MILF is, quite simply, polite society's "hot mom."

Is that an oxymoron? It shouldn't be.

For thousands of years, women were expected to hang up their "hotness" once they had children. On the rare occasion someone was bold enough to refer to a mom as "sexy," they would do so at the expense of her children, mentioning them as an afterthought, a caveat or disclaimer.

"That woman sure is hot, BUT she has kids. . . ."

Why should it be that the instant a woman gives birth she is suddenly undesirable? I am willing to concede that a woman is perhaps less than sexually desirable *while* she's giving birth, but really, shouldn't that be the parameter? Once she's ceased screaming like a banshee and she's back in her recovery room, she looks kind of cute in that hospital gown— and it is open in back.

After all, having kids doesn't put an end to your hotness; it enhances it. Seriously, if there weren't any MILFs, we would *all* be only children.

The modern mom isn't defined by society's expectations. She wears clothes that make her feel great; she shows off her pregnant belly; she savors life, is ambitious, focused and so much more—she is a MILF. She hasn't stopped living.

And the MILF movement continues to grow. MILFs are everywhere. They're in the media, in the fashion industry, all over TV and in the movies. Society has redefined and rallied around motherhood like never before. Today's mom makes her family a priority, but she still finds time to care for herself and do what's necessary to maintain her sense of humor and, of course, her sanity.

There's no doubt about it: MILF is the new black.

And they are more prominent than ever before. Everywhere you look, in fact—the tabloids, television, the White House—you see examples of MILFs: celebrities like Heidi Klum, Gwyneth Paltrow, Salma Hayek, Jessica Alba, Brooke Shields, Sandra Bullock, Gwen Stefani, Halle Berry and Jennifer Lopez traipse across the tabloids toting their tots; Michelle Obama, Sarah Palin and Arianna Huffington have given the political landscape some beautiful curves; and women like Tina Fey, Patricia Heaton and Téa Leoni have stylishly shown that one of the sexiest parts of a mom is her funny bone. . . .

These women are hot. And it could be said that it is precisely the juxtaposition of their hotness against the backdrop of their families and careers that makes them even more intriguing. The image of any beautiful, confident woman surrounded by her grabby leprechauns makes her look even more gorgeous and accessible—hence "hotter." Men can't help but see a woman like this and think, *Wow, she looks great. . . . I'd f@#k her*—the F in the acronym MILF standing for the ultimate compliment a man can pay a woman. Why? Because when a man says, "I'd f@#k her," it is the equivalent of him saying, "She is so beautiful, I would like to recite to her a sonnet." "I'd f@#k her" is just easier, less time-consuming, and usually results in way more high fives with their buddies than sonnet recitation.

Alternately, women see that same mom with her brood, packed into her minivan or walking around the market, and think, *Wow, she looks great. . . . F@#k her!*—the F in MILF translating into the equally complimentary: "She's really pretty and I like her highlights. Damn her for having such great skin and I really hate how those jeans really make her ass look so good. Oh sure, look at her hugging her kid. I bet he just threw a huge tantrum. Ha! Why the hell is she smiling? . . . I hate her." Again, "F@#k her" is just easier and less time-consuming.

It's easy to look at celebrity moms and think, *Well, of course they look great! They have a hairstylist and makeup artist living in the back of their car; expensive chefs cook them nutritious low-fat, low-carb, gluten-free meals; and they have, like, twelve nannies.* That could be. In fact, it very well might be. But here's the thing: these MILFs may be armed with mascara and a personal trainer, but there is something they share with all MILFs—rich or poor, old or young, skinny or full-figured—and that's attitude. You can't buy it, you can't fake it, and just because you're famous doesn't mean you can get it for free in an Oscar swag bag. Attitude, class and style are integral to being super MILFy, and they only come from one place: inside. MILFs don't sweat the small stuff. Sure, they get knocked over and sometimes crack. Who doesn't? But it takes a certain amount of savoir faire and je ne sais quoi to maintain your appeal while having a nervous breakdown, don't you think?

Finally, MILFs have one thing their pre-maternal sisters will never have—something special that screams out to every man we pass, whether we are pushing an English pram or pulling a screaming toddler. This fact is universal to all MILFs, undeniable and eminently attractive to men. MILFs put out. And they're the only ones who can prove it.

Now, that's hot.

the MILF
vs.
the cougar

> I don't want to be a cougar . . . ,
> I want to be a MILF! I hate that word
> "cougar" and what it represents.
> "MILF" is a word I absolutely love.

—CINDY CRAWFORD IN AN INTERVIEW
WITH BRITAIN'S *GQ* MAGAZINE

Maybe you're thinking, *A MILF, a cougar . . . same thing.* Don't be fooled. A MILF is most definitely *not* a cougar. Many women over thirty-five would rebuke and kick any man in the nuts for calling them a cougar. (I certainly would.) It's insulting. Cougars are tightly clad, aggressive, youth-obsessed creatures. They prowl for sex, they prowl for conquests and they're ever on the prowl for confirmation that they've "still got it."

Need an example? Remember Anne Bancroft in *The Graduate*? She had such an impact on audiences that even today people still use the term "Mrs. Robinson" when they describe a desirable, lusty and extremely saucy, married (albeit adulterous) woman. This is exactly the kind of image that gives MILFs a bad name. News flash: Mrs. Robinson was NOT a MILF. She was a cougar.

A MILF doesn't need to prove she's "still got it"; she has more important things to do. Like manage a household, juggle her responsibilities (inside and outside the home) and raise a family. A MILF is confident, ambivalent to judgment and in charge of her life. She is loved because she can give love, she is adored because she knows how to make others feel adored, and people want to be near her because she is thoughtful, confident and *really* cute jumping up and down on the sidelines of the soccer field cheering for her kid.

The fact is cougars have begun a cultural backslide from which they will never recover, whereas the MILF is back, better than ever, and here to stay.

And why?

Because . . .

- Being called a MILF is a compliment. Being called a cougar is not. . . .
- A MILF comes in all shapes and sizes. A cougar does not. . . .
- A MILF is pursued and adored. A cougar prowls and conquers.
- A MILF has children. A cougar dates "children."
- A MILF ages gracefully. A cougar, well . . . it's just sad.

My point is, in a death match, a MILF would kick cougar butt.

I have an idea that the phrase "weaker sex" was coined by some woman to disarm some man she was preparing to overwhelm.

—OGDEN NASH

MILF is cool, MILF is refreshing, and MILF is delicious with chocolate cake. MILFs simply endure the test of time and have lasting power.

But most important, MILFdom is infinitely more indicative of where the modern woman has taken motherhood. The new incarnation of MILF is about embracing the whole woman. Being sexier, savvier, more beautiful *because* you have children, not *despite* them.

Ask anyone. MILFs rule!

anatomy of a MILF

1. **SHOES:** flats, or some other comfortable but chic little shoe

2. **HANDBAG:** big and overstuffed

3. **CONTENTS IN HANDBAG:** wipes, water and old tissues, expired coupons, extra gift cards in case you forgot some kid's birthday party, gum, and candy to bribe young children

4. **CELL PHONE:** always out in case one of your kids missed their ride

5. **SHOPPING BAG:** kids' clothes (sale at GapKids)

6. **CLOTHING:** simple, elegant and in layers so if a kid spills juice, wipes their cream cheese fingers on you or sneezes on your cardigan, you can just "peel" and move on to the next fresh layer

7. **UNDERWEAR:** Hanky Panky or Cosabella thong. MILFs don't tolerate panty lines.

8. **EARRINGS:** diamond studs or simple gold posts that can't be grabbed, snagged or pulled

9. **SUNGLASSES:** protect from UV rays and hide the puffy eyes you have from being woken up in the middle of the night to take a kid, or two, to the bathroom

10. **HAIR:** possibly clean and pulled off face into a ponytail

11. **NAILS:** au naturel or short and polished; toes may need retouching since your son stepped on your fresh pedicure

12. **CLEAVAGE:** natural, but decorated with a charm necklace containing your kid's initials or a diamond that was your "push present"

13. **SINGLE STANDOUT ACCESSORY:** gives the impression "I tried"

14. **FAVORITE ACCESSORY:** small child who looks like you

anatomy of a cougar

1. **SHOES**: spiky heels at all times. Even the playground. Can you push a swing in four-inch stilettos? I can't.

2. **HANDBAG**: big and metallic

3. **CONTENTS IN HANDBAG**: stuffed with credit cards, condoms and lip plumper. She also has candy in bag . . . to lure young boys.

4. **CELL PHONE**: always out, ready to reply to booty call

5. **SHOPPING BAG**: pricey designer dress for clubbing

6. **CLOTHING**: flamboyant, trendy (For the record, grape jelly and white chinchilla just don't mix.)

7. **UNDERWEAR**: none

8. **EARRINGS**: hoops. Don't let the kids grab them.

9. **SUNGLASSES**: hide puffiness from a heavy night of partying; often worn indoors

10. **HAIR**: big, wild. Even though it looks natural, it took hours to do just right.

11. **SPRAY TAN**

12. **NAILS**: long; acrylic or press-on. They're badass.

13. **CLEAVAGE**: usually bedecked with something big and sparkly to distract you from sun damage

14. **FAVORITE ACCESSORY**: small dog that looks like her

CHAPTER THREE

MILFs
throughout
history

> **The woman is weak,
> but the mother is strong.**
>
> —KOREAN PROVERB

MILFs have always been around. If you look across cultures and throughout time, you see the women who were simply thought of as captivating (not only because of their physical attributes, but also because of what they accomplished), when, really, these women were very MILFy—from Cleopatra to Princess Diana. These women broke from the societal bonds and standards of their time to pursue their passions and get dinner on the table for their hungry broods. Though they likely broke a nail, stained a shirt or ruined a fresh blow-dry along the way, they managed to stay beautiful and confident, and maintain a sense of poise as they built pyramids, ruled kingdoms and checked other items off their to-do lists.

Today's MILFs are just as admired as their historical sisters. They are in charge. They're strong. And they, too, embrace age and motherhood and remain icons of beauty and magnetism. Their sexuality has not been camouflaged by such motherly accoutrements as the pageboy or "mom jeans"—such style choices conspiring to turn even the most beautiful woman into an Amish hausfrau, thus sapping her of any tangible sexuality.

Even in ancient Egypt, I highly doubt that Nefertiti would have chopped off her own beautiful hair just so she could deal with her kids' rampant lice issues. She would have just piled it up, pinning it under her Nubian wig with some emerald and ruby hair clips, and set to the task of picking out the nits herself. Okay, she succumbed to the plague eventually, but that was only because she was probably the one holding her little ones' heads while they puked.

---

*If evolution really works, how come
mothers only have two hands?*

— MILTON BERLE

Being a MILF hasn't gotten any easier. Despite the fact that for thousands of years MILFs were out in the hot desert sun herding sheep, on farms tilling fields, churning butter, building families, and cleaning up after plagues, the challenges a modern MILF faces today are just as grueling; chauffeuring a minivan full of screaming children from one activity to the next (. . . and the next . . . and the next . . .); prepping kids for exams our ancestors would have failed miserably; finding and preparing food for your family that won't poison them; staving off swine flu; maintaining a successful career; and finding time for sex with your husband despite the new HBO lineup. Today's MILF conquers these tasks and more—and all without their families in the tent next door.

MILFs have withstood the tests of time. We've evolved. We are a testament to Darwin's theory of "survival of the fittest," and as long as there are kids to care for, passions to pursue and friends to feast with, we will continue to thrive.

It would seem that something which means poverty, disorder and violence every single day should be avoided entirely. But the desire to beget children is a natural urge.

—PHYLLIS DILLER

MILF Duds

Of course, for as long as there have been MILFs, there have also been MILF Duds. Moms who prioritize EVERYONE above themselves or—just as sadly—prioritize themselves above all others. The MILF Dud is so concerned with how the outside world sees her that she doesn't even recognize herself or her own needs. Worry cloaks her. Fear paralyzes her. Original thought eludes her.

There is no balance with the MILF Dud. How can you be hot when you don't even know who you are? The MILF Dud's passions, needs and wants are put aside for everyone else's. And by doing this, the MILF Dud takes no responsibility. Certainly not for herself and her own life.

Or, conversely, she sees *only* herself. She competes with her children for attention and feels "alive" only when other people are talking to her or talking about her. She is a shadow, defined only by the light around her. When the spotlight isn't on her, she doesn't exist. She sees herself only via how others view her. She clings to other people and to youth. And by doing so, she denies herself the one thing she wants most— the ability to love life.

Notable MILFs Throughout History

Nefertiti (1370 BC–1330 BC): Royal wife of a pharaoh, leader of a religious revolution and mother of six girls (and five hundred cats). That's a lot of cat-fighting!

Bathsheba (approximately 1020 BC–approximately 980 BC): She was already married when she met King David, who was mesmerized by her beauty and killed her husband so he could marry her himself. Together, they had four sons.

Cleopatra (69 BC–30 BC): Queen of Egypt, lover of Mark Antony and mother of four (including twins!). Very MILFy. Then she committed suicide. Not so MILFy.

Wang Zhaojun (approximately 31 BC–1 BC): One of the famed "Four Beauties of China," she had two sons and a daughter with her first husband, and was then commanded by levirate custom (in which case a man has to marry his dead brother's widow) to marry her stepson and gave him two daughters.

Queen Victoria (1819–1901): She was renowned for her iron will and was barely eighteen when she became the Queen of England. She fell in love with and married her cousin Prince Albert. They could barely keep their hands off each other and had nine children: four sons and five daughters. Little known fact: Queen Victoria is responsible for the tradition of brides wearing white for their weddings.

Coretta Scott King (1927–2006): Wife of Martin Luther King Jr., civil rights crusader and mother of four. She was also an accomplished singer; she created and performed concerts about the civil rights movement.

Jacqueline Kennedy Onassis (1929–1994): Wife of the thirty-fifth president of the United States, John F. Kennedy, mother of two and inimitable style icon. Who doesn't adore those black-and-white photos of her playing with Caroline and John Jr.? She's gorgeous in those pearls.

Grace Kelly (1929–1982): The iconic American beauty who married Prince Rainier of Monaco and became princess consort of Monaco. She had three children: Caroline, Albert and Stéphanie. Grace Kelly is perhaps one of the most iconic MILFs of all time. Beautiful, poised, gracious, loving, warm, talented . . . and let's not even get started on the accessories. *Très* MILFy.

Queen Noor of Jordan (born 1951): The queen is the last wife and widow of King Hussein of Jordan. She is a stepmother to three children from the king's marriage to Queen Alia, and had four more children with her husband. She is the current president of the United World Colleges movement and an advocate of the anti–nuclear weapons proliferation campaign Global Zero. That's one busy MILF.

Benazir Bhutto (1953–2007): Mother of two girls and one boy from an arranged marriage, she was the first woman ever to be elected prime minister of Pakistan. A year after she was assassinated, she was one of seven winners of the United Nations Prize in the Field of Human Rights. She was a SUPER MILF!

Carol Brady (aka Mrs. Brady, aka Florence Henderson): Yes, she's fictional, but you can't have a list of MILFs throughout history without mentioning the first truly MILFy mom on television ever! She was hot for her husband, he was hot for her, and they slept in the same bed. Shocking! And Florence Henderson has four kids of her own in real life.

Notable MILF Duds Throughout History

Helen of Troy: Yeah, yeah . . . her face launched a thousand ships. We get it. . . . She was pretty. But (mythical or not) few people know that Helen had a daughter, Hermione, by her husband, Menelaus, and ditched her when she left Sparta for Troy with Paris. Very un-MILFy.

Agrippina the Younger (AD 15–AD 59): She is said to have murdered her second husband in order to bring her son, Nero, to the throne. That worked out well for her . . . not.

Isabella of Castile/Queen Isabella (1451–1504): This queen of Spain started "the Spanish Inquisition." Talk about intolerant. Intolerance is not MILFy.

Mata Hari (1876–1917): The infamous Dutch exotic dancer who was executed by the French as a spy. Her name is synonymous with espionage. Although she was married, she had many lovers and was known for her willingness to be almost naked onstage. Lying, cheating, debauchery—Mata Hari was obviously a cougar.

Joan Crawford (1905–1977): This "mommie dearest" may be remembered best not for her acting career but for her obsessive, abusive nature and a pet peeve for wire hangers.

Dina Lohan (born 1962): Ah yes. Leeching off your child's fame to her detriment, and using it as a stepping stool to your own. She and Kate Gosselin should be introduced.

Michelle Duggar (born 1966): For having more children than square footage. Oh wait. . . . I think she just had another. . . .

Pamela Anderson (born 1967): Made it to twenty-one and decided she never wanted to age one more second. We can thank Pam for showing us exactly how unattractive Peter Pan syndrome can be.

Kate Gosselin (born 1975): Temper tantrums, obsession with fame, and the inability to convince anyone that her children are a priority and not just a meal ticket. But the most disturbing parenting trait? The way she dresses all of her kids alike.

The "Octomom" (born 1975): For intentionally stuffing more embryos into her uterus than marshmallows in the mouth of a Cub Scout with a sensory integration disorder (and with just as much forethought). Don't even get me started on that laugh of hers. . . .

celebrity MILFs

Michelle Obama
Jennifer Lopez
Brooke Burke
Sofia Vergara
Gwen Stefani
Salma Hayek
Reese Witherspoon
Kourtney Kardashian
Jessica Alba
Padma Lakshmi
Sarah Jessica Parker
Sarah Palin
Angelina Jolie
Jada Pinkett Smith
Brooke Shields
Demi Moore
Arianna Huffington
Tina Fey
Uma Thurman
Catherine Zeta-Jones

Halle Berry
Cindy Crawford
Nora Ephron
Gabrielle Reece
Vanessa Williams
Jennifer Garner
Faith Hill
Elle Macpherson
Tina Turner
Kate Winslet
Rebecca Romijn
Julianne Moore
Julia Louis-Dreyfus
Susan Sarandon
Tori Spelling
Sheryl Crow
Gwyneth Paltrow
Nicole Richie
Madonna

celebrity MILF duds

Britney Spears
Kate Gosselin
"Octomom"
Kirstie Alley
Jamie Spears
Pamela Anderson

Dina Lohan
Linda Hogan
Kimora Lee Simmons
Any mom who loses all
    her baby weight in six
    weeks or less

the many varieties of MILF

One of the best things about MILFs? MILFs come in all shapes, sizes, colors and flavors. Find the one that's right for you.

1. **Breast MILF** (aka *The Breast-Feeding MILF*): The Breast MILF is just settling into her routine as a mom and finding her rhythm (which, coincidentally, may also be her birth control). With her healthy body, buoyant breasts and "nurturing" air, this MILF has found her groove. Is it any wonder there are so many siblings only a year or two apart? (NOTE: Rhythm method = more babies.)

2. **Chocolate MILF** (aka *The Outgoing MILF*): Everyone loves Chocolate MILF. She's simply delicious and goes

with everything. And what's not to love? Looking fabulous even when she's just picking her kid up from playgroup, the Chocolate MILF is a stylish, personable, multitasking machine. Able to hold a conversation with her friends AND keep her kids from running out into traffic, this MILF makes it look like she has it all under control. She volunteers at school, is a fabulous cook and can make anyone feel comfortable with her smile alone. This MILF is smooth, delicious and always a treat.

3. **Coconut MILF** (aka *The Nutty MILF*): This MILF is a bit bonkers, but that's okay. She simply dances to the beat of her own drummer (and we can't hear it). She loves people, loves to travel and makes even the dullest party more interesting (if she can remember when it is). She's wacky, full of life and adds flavor wherever she goes.

4. **Curdled MILF** (aka *The MILF Gone Bad*): When friendships go south, and anger and bad feelings linger, you're left with Curdled MILF. See "Curdled MILF: When Friendship Expires . . ." in Chapter 12 for more on this subject.

5. **Expired MILF** (aka *The Perpetually Late MILF*): She's late for dinners, late for meetings, and often has to call upon fellow MILFs to ask them to explain to her kid that she's running late for pickup. Maybe she has too much on her plate, maybe she lost track of time, but it happens

constantly and it's a bit unsavory. And while she may look fresh when she *finally* arrives, no one really enjoys MILF once it expires. It just loses some of its appeal. This MILF is found primarily in Los Angeles and other Southern California locations including Orange County, Beverly Hills and Newport Beach.

6. **Fresh MILF** (aka *The New MILF*): Maybe she's been home with her newborn for six weeks wondering when the H#LL this screaming baby will "latch on," or maybe she's just back in her hospital room after pushing for three hours. Either way, she's flushed in the face, filled with love (when not totally exhausted), and her boobs are enormous.

7. **Homogenized MILF** (aka *The Medically Enhanced MILF*): This MILF has had a little "freshening." "Touching up" is a part of this MILF's beauty routine (a *dash* of Botox here, a little Restylane there, maybe even a little under-eye work if they get really puffy). But face-lift, after face-lift (. . . after boob job, after tummy tuck, after lip injections, after lipo . . .) is not. This MILF is possibly too focused on looking good, but at least understands you're not MILFy if you can't register any emotion other than surprise . . . or pucker.

8. **Organic MILF** (aka *The Urbane Version of the Soy MILF*): This MILF likes to keep it natural—especially when

it comes to her kids. She buys organic food, recycles plastic bottles and hits the farmers' market every Sunday in search of fresh arugula and kettle corn. She's strong-willed and environmentally conscious, and can usually be found volunteering at her kid's school or carpooling to karate in a Prius.

9. **Pasteurized MILF (aka *The Menopausal MILF*):** You don't need to have young babies to be a MILF. Look at Helen Mirren, Blythe Danner and Barbara Bush. . . . (I threw that last one in there to see if you were paying attention. . . . She's actually not very MILFy—frankly, it's the hair.) They've survived raising kids, the heat of menopause and the pull of gravity with grace and beauty, and continue to live their lives to the fullest. These gorgeous women are proof that you can move past your childbearing years but STILL be in your prime!

10. **Raw MILF (aka *The MILF au Naturel*):** A MILF who just got out of the shower.

11. **Single Serving of MILF (aka *The Single MILF*):** Whether she has one child or three, this single mother makes her family feel whole and complete.

12. **Soy MILF (aka *The Vegetarian/Vegan MILF*):** A hippie at heart, the Soy MILF is not a conformer and can often be found at (or leading) rallies to free third-world countries (or discussing their plight in her acceptance speech). She's

a healthy eater, a yoga practitioner, and uses whole wheat bread and natural peanut butter in her children's lunches. This MILF likes to keep it "natural." That being said, the Soy MILF understands hairy armpits are a big no-no.

13. **Spilled MILF** (aka *The MILF All Over the Floor*): Life as a mom is hard and we all, at one time or another, get knocked over. No one expects perfection. But the great thing about Spilled MILF is that you don't need to cry over it (not for long). With a little help, you can clean it up and be as fresh as ever.

14. **Spoiled MILF** (aka *The MILF Imposter*): This MILF *looks* like a MILF from far away—she's attractive, confident, seems nice enough—but once you get a little closer (you know, take a whiff and perhaps venture a taste), you realize you've been duped. The Spoiled MILF is self-centered, arrogant, and has little if no interest in anything that doesn't directly involve her. Spending time with her is just no fun. In fact, it leaves a bad taste in your mouth . . . and might just make you want to throw up.

15. **Steamed MILF** (aka *The "Don't Cross Her" MILF*): A MILF whose kid was supposed to be picked up for basketball by another mom but wasn't, or whose kid just put his peanut-buttery fingers all over her favorite new shirt, or who just found lipstick on her husband's collar . . .

16. **MILF Dud:** A mom who hasn't embraced her inner MILF. She is so concerned with how her family and the outside world see her that she doesn't recognize herself or her own needs. Or, conversely, she prioritizes herself at the expense of her family. Either way, this dud lacks confidence, balance and perspective, and just can't enjoy her own life. The MILF Dud can be identified by the wake of blame trailing behind her and an inappropriate hairdo.

(CHAPTER FIVE)

are you a MILF?

TEST YOUR MILF QUOTIENT

> One is not born a woman
> but becomes one.

—SIMONE DE BEAUVOIR, *THE SECOND SEX*, 1949

So now you have a basic understanding of what it means to be a MILF, but the burning question remains: "Just how MILFy am I?" Take this quiz to find out! Read each question and choose the answer that best describes how you would respond:

1. **You get an invitation to an acquaintance's party. Your husband is out of town on business and can't go with you. You:**

   a. go, of course. Being solo at a party is not a problem, even if you don't know anyone.

   b. decline and make up an excuse. You don't want your friend to know you feel uncomfortable coming without your spouse.

c. ask your hostess who else is going that you might know so you can make arrangements to come with another guest. If you don't know anyone else going, you decline.

2. **You're exhausted and have a headache, but it's just you with the kids all night and you haven't even made dinner. You:**

a. order in, leave the cartons on the table with silverware and hang a note on your door that says, "Do Not Disturb." Hopefully, they'll eventually go to sleep and you'll clean up the mess tomorrow.

b. celebrate "Bad Mommy Night," in which you let the kids eat cereal for dinner and you all watch bad movies in your bed together.

c. throw frozen dinners into the oven and scream at your kids all night. After all, who gave you the headache in the first place?

d. force yourself to make dinner and hold it together till bedtime for the kids' sake.

3. **What best describes how you spend your extra time?**

a. What extra time? You're up to your eyeballs in car pool and PTA. There's no time for you.

b. You hug the nanny hello, pat the children and make a beeline for the tennis club.

c. You have the nanny or babysitter come once a week in the evenings so you can take just one photography or landscaping class. Your brain is going to mush!

d. You find part-time child care so you can spend a couple afternoons a week doing something for you.

4. **Your child's school spring show is tomorrow morning, but you just got a notice that your favorite designer is having a sample sale and the doors open at the same time. You:**

   a. miss the recital. We're talkin' 80 percent off!

   b. miss the sale.

   c. get to the sale really early and miss the first half of your child's show.

5. **You need to go to the market, but you've just been to the gym, look like you got run over with a treadmill and don't have time to go home and shower before you have to pick up the kids from school. You:**

   a. ditch the market and pray you can make something for dinner out of chickpeas and Hamburger Helper.

b. go to the market, but hide your hideousness by crouching in the condiment aisle when you see someone you know in fresh fruit.

c. take on the market, sweaty clothes and all. You see someone you know in the fresh fruit aisle and you say hello . . . forgoing the kiss, of course.

6. **Which best describes your sex life?**

a. You have sex three or more times a week.

b. You have sex once a week.

c. Sex? Is that when the man puts his penis in your vagina?

7. **Which best describes your underwear drawer?**

a. It's overflowing with underwear you've had since college . . . possibly before. They have no elasticity and holes in the wrong places.

b. You have varying levels of underwear: period underwear (the crappy stuff with some holes), daily underwear (passable if seen by a friend at the gym), and date-night underwear (three to five pairs of the good stuff).

c. You have lots of sexy lingerie. What isn't "sexy" is at least in great condition.

8. **You just found out from your crying child that he/she didn't get the solo in the school chorus. You respond by:**

   a. marching into the music director's office and ripping him/her a new asshole. It doesn't change anything, but you feel better.

   b. marching into the music director's office and bribing him/her. It works.

   c. consoling your child and telling him/her there is always next year.

   d. consoling your child and suggesting he/she go back to the music director and ask him/her to let your child audition again.

9. **You are offered a wine list at a restaurant. Your husband/date admits he doesn't know wines. You:**

   a. play dumb. You don't want to hurt his pride. So you order the house zinfandel.

   b. ask for suggestions from the sommelier.

   c. ask for "the fresh stuff."

d. tell the sommelier to bring you a glass of the Montepulciano d'Abruzzo. You've had it before, remembered the name and vintage, and loved it.

10. **A good-looking stranger smiles at you while you're with your child/ren. You:**

a. look him straight in the eye and smile back. You lock eyes.

b. smile back and walk on.

c. look away quickly. That's so wrong; you're with your kids.

d. look at your feet.

11. **Regarding oral sex:**

a. Ew! Never.

b. You're a giver.

c. You're a getter.

d. Sixty-nine is at the top of your list.

12. **How do you like your sex?**

a. sweet and gentle with very little variation

b. rough and hard . . . "Who was that guy?"

c. You're not a gymnast or anything, but you keep your old Halloween costumes around "just for fun."

13. **You are at a friend's fortieth birthday party and your husband/partner is feeling a little "frisky." You:**

a. slap his hand away.

b. whisper, "Later," in his ear and wink.

c. grab your man and find a powder room—fast!

14. **Your children are finally in preschool. After years of being home with them, you find you have the mornings free. You:**

a. pursue a hobby or interest.

b. exercise and meet friends for coffee.

c. clean your house. A mom's work is never done.

d. watch TV.

15. **When you're in line at the market, which magazine are you most likely to flip through?**

a. *Vanity Fair*

b. *National Enquirer*

c. *Ladies' Home Journal*

d. *People*

16. **You need shoes for a party where you know there will be music and dancing, so you:**

a. wear a pair of stilettos that make your legs look really toned and long. You can't dance, but you'll sure look hot sitting down.

b. buy a pair of practical flats.

c. buy a nice pair of heels that aren't so high they'll kill you. When they start to bother you, you take them off and dance barefoot.

d. buy a nice pair of heels that aren't so high they'll kill you. When they start to bother you, you sit the rest of the night out.

17. **You and your husband have been fighting a lot lately. You:**

a. cheat on your spouse at the first opportunity. He doesn't appreciate you.

b. cheat on your spouse only after you wait for things to get better and they don't.

c. talk to your spouse about the problem. If that doesn't work, you seek counseling.

d. look up old boyfriends on Facebook and resent your spouse till you explode like a raging volcano.

18. **You are a married working mom. You're away on a business trip and you are really horny. You:**

a. find a discreet coworker and f@#k his brains out.

b. stare at the ceiling all night.

c. pleasure yourself.

d. have phone sex with your husband.

19. **You wax:**

a. your entire bikini line. Clean as the day God made you.

b. only the edges of your bikini line. Keeping it "natural."

c. actually, you don't.

d. just about everything. You're a Brazilian babe from the waist down. Clean with a small "landing strip."

20. **You're at a high school reunion. You see an old boy-friend who "can't believe how great you look." You:**

   a. flirt the whole evening whenever your husband isn't watching.

   b. take him upstairs in the hotel. After all, you came alone.

   c. hug your husband's arm, smile and say thank you!

   d. kiss your old boyfriend and say thank you right in front of your husband.

What Is Your MILF Quotient?
Quiz Answer Key

Find the point value that corresponds to each answer you chose. When you have completed making a list of your answers and their point values, add up your points. Your total reflects your MILF quotient, which is defined on pages 52–54.

1. a) 3   b) 0   c) 1

2. a) 1   b) 3   c) 0   d) 1

3. a) 0   b) 1   c) 3   d) 2

4. a) 0   b) 3   c) 1

5. a) 0   b) 1   c) 3

6. a) 3   b) 2   c) 0

7. a) 0   b) 2   c) 3

8. a) 0   b) 1   c) 3   d) 2

9. a) 0   b) 3   c) 0   d) 3

10. a) 2   b) 3   c) 0   d) 0

11. a) 0   b) 2   c) 1   d) 3

12. a) 1   b) 1   c) 3

13. a) 0   b) 3   c) 3

14. a) 3   b) 2   c) 1   d) 0

15. a) 3   b) 3   c) 3   d) 3

16. a) 1   b) 1   c) 3   d) 2

17. a) 0   b) 0   c) 3   d) 2

18. a) 0   b) 0   c) 1   d) 3

19. a) 1   b) 2   c) 0   d) 3

20. a) 1   b) 0   c) 3   d) 2

What your score says about you:

46–60: 100% WHOLE MILF—You are confident in your choices, comfortable with who you are, and you don't let petty issues get you down. And while your world does not revolve around looking good, you know how to pull yourself together and stand out in a crowd. No stranger to flirting, be it with your husband, boyfriend or the policeman who wants to give you a ticket for illegally turning left out of a Starbucks, motherhood has not sapped you of your sex drive. Your family means the world to you and you would do anything for them. You coddle but you don't spoil. You're accessible but you don't lose yourself to them either. You have lots of outside interests and know that a "happy mom" means a "happy family." Fueling yourself means having more to give your kids. You know that how you look on the outside is a reflection of how you feel about yourself on the inside—and you feel f@#king fantastic. That being said, while you like looking good, you're not hung up on perfection. You have a life, after all, and who has the time? To you, being happy and looking good means feeling good and taking care of yourself. If you happen to look fabulous in the process? Well, that's an added benefit. While you might be tempted into some minor physical "tweaks" as time goes on, you would never resort to major plastic surgery. Trying to freeze yourself in time is not beautiful to you.

26–45: LOWFAT MILF—Maybe you're still mired in the murkiness of early motherhood, maybe you just haven't fully embraced the beauty that is you, or maybe it's a little of both. You have a lot of spirit brimming under your unshowered surface and you're itching to shout out, "I'm still in here!" You second-guess your choices more than you should and allow yourself to feel unattractive. You need to learn how to embrace your inner MILF. Maybe it'll take some time, or maybe all you need is a good cup of tea and a long hot shower (with the doors locked!). If you're a working mom, maybe you're still trying to find that balance between work and family. Good luck! Even when we're working "in the home," it's impossible to find a way to make everyone happy. So get over it! It's all right to not have the answers. No one expects you to, except maybe your kids, and eventually they'll figure out you don't know everything anyway. You're still getting your feet wet when it comes to finding yourself, and that's all right. You could also simply be so overwhelmed by motherhood right now that you just couldn't find "you" if you were hit in the face with "you." That's all right. You'll figure it all out soon enough, and with the help of this book, you're on your way.

5–25: SKIM MILF—You are definitely not tapping into your full MILF potential. Maybe you're too concerned that everyone else is judging you. Maybe you think your world has to be your kids or you're not a good mom. Maybe you feel like you just can't handle any of it. Well, I'm here to tell you, you're NOT ALONE! We all feel that way sometimes. But the difference between a MILF and a MILF Dud is the confidence that you are doing the best you can and the belief that you are a great wife, mother and "you"! You still need to find yourself, and with a little help, you can! But if we come out there and find you sitting and watching soap opera reruns in your "mom jeans" and slippers, we're going to be very upset.

the
MILF
container

THE MILF AND HER CAR

A suburban mother's role
is to deliver children obstetrically
once, and by car forever after.

—PETER DE VRIES

What's a MILF without her minivan, SUV or hybrid? I'll tell you what she is—she's *some* lady on a street corner wondering how she's going to drop the kids off at school, swing by the post office, then get to her office, then get to Pilates, pick up the dog at the groomer's, get her kids to karate, then baseball, then ballet, make it all the way across town to the salon to get her hair colored, and be home in time to make dinner.

Unless a MILF lives in a big city and uses public transportation, she needs a car. Badly. Without it she can't drive car pool, take her kids to school or get her twenty bags of groceries home from the market. The MILF's car is her appendage . . . her office . . . her second home.

By taking a close look at this most private, personal and

intimate corner of a MILF's life, you can see how MILFs really live. Their cars reveal their passions (music, audiobooks, tennis, frozen yogurt), foibles (gum chewing, overdue library books, more frozen yogurt), idiosyncrasies (extra underwear for everyone, gallons of hand sanitizer, more frozen yogurt) and secrets (a frozen yogurt obsession). We learn more about the MILF from dissecting her "container" than from all other sources put together.

A MILF Pimps Her Ride

A MILF is practical, but never so without style. One of the best lines I ever heard was from my sister (a proud MILF), who called from the car dealership to tell me she was "succumbing to life with a minivan," then added, ". . . but I got it totally pimped out!" Images of flames painted across the automatic sliding side doors of her Sienna flashed through my mind. Maybe a shiny chrome muffler sticking out. Or it played a tangy little tune when you honked?

I wondered—can you pimp a minivan? Apparently, you can. And it's pretty f@#king awesome! You can have **satellite radio** and even choose a family-friendly package; a **navigation system** so you never get lost again (just for fun, you can ignore the bossy lady telling you where to go and listen to her say, "Recalculating . . ." over and over. She never gets mad. That's really cool.); a **reverse-sensing system** and a **rearview camera** that come with an irritating beep that gets more and more rapid as you get closer and closer to an object behind you; **electric side-window sunshades** that used to be found only in luxury sedans and offer instant shade at the touch of a button; **in-floor storage** so your groceries don't have to sit out in the sun anymore and are out of the way; a **separate audio system** so when you can't listen to Raffi for one more minute, the kids can have their own audio system complete with headphones (It's quite possible you may never have to hear "Baby Beluga" ever again.); **seat warmers** for toasty buns; a **115-volt power outlet**, which may mean nothing to you except that now you have a STANDARD household outlet in the car and could plug in a PlayStation (woo-hoo!); **power-down rear-side windows** so there's no more fishbowl effect and there's fresh air for all; a **table** for those kids who want to play a board game on a long ride (BONUS: So passengers can use the table, the middle seats face *away* from you!); a **rear DVD entertainment system** (videos and earphones = quiet children. Need I say more?).

But are you ready for the ultimate in minivan pimpage? Onboard hard drive: some minivans have the capacity to store several thousand music files and several dozen movies in the car! No more goopy CDs.

What's next, autopilot?

what's in a MILF's car?

1. **PORTABLE GYMNASIUM**: tennis racquets, lacrosse sticks, soccer ball, extra karate gi and sparring gear, baseball bat, ball and glove, free weights (two and three pounds) and stretch ribbon—in case you can squeeze in a walk between errands and school pickup—and necessary changes of clothing and footwear for all potential activities

2. **BLOOMINGDALE'S, NORDSTROM OR NEIMAN MARCUS SHOPPING BAG**: containing something really cute and most likely highly unnecessary, along with the receipt in case buyer's remorse sets in and a return is in order

3. **BLOOMINGDALE'S, NORDSTROM OR NEIMAN MARCUS SHOPPING BAG**: containing cute T-shirts and pants you won't be returning. (NOTE: If you're a MILF with daughters, this bag is either tucked in the trunk/back of the car, or under the front seat so as to curtail rifling, pilfering and/or reports of shopping back to their father.)

4. **EXTRA BOOSTER SEAT**: in case of unplanned carpooling

5. **4,500 CALORIES' WORTH OF SNACKS**: Usually packed in ice, this bag contains all of the nutritious snacks you could ever need if you went on a road trip across the country . . . and back. This bag usually contains probiotic bars, cereal snack bars, pretzels, Goldfish (two or more varieties), drinkable yogurt, cut carrots, cut apples, cut-up pieces of some kind of fruit you don't normally get, but it was on sale and you thought it would provide a little novelty to your kids, who are sick of apples and carrots. Plus tiny dip containers that make eating apples and carrots "fun" but invariably spill.

6. **ROLL OF PAPER TOWELS**: usually wedged under one of the seats

7. **VALET PARKING TICKET STUB**: from the mall last week. It's still on your windshield.

8. **BOOKS FOR THE LIBRARY**: three months overdue at least

9. **EXTRA SWEATSHIRT**: just in case of emergencies. Unfortunately, it's so dirty from sitting in the car for so long that no one will wear it.

10. **BAG OF CLOTHES YOUR KIDS HAVE OUTGROWN**: for Goodwill. It's been in your car for more than six months.

11. **RECEIPTS**: for gas, for McDonald's (where you had to stop when your kids wouldn't eat the carrots and apples), from the post office from when you mailed your nephew's birthday present two months late

12. **LOOSE CDS**: covered in some kind of mysterious sticky filth

13. **DRIED PENS**: none of them work

14. **IN-CAR PHONE CHARGER**: for your last phone, which dropped down a toilet at the preschool. This charger does not work on your new phone.

15. **PADS AND PADS OF PAPER**: most likely from some neighborhood real estate agent who left them on your doorstep in hopes you might move. Like, now.

16. **FLASHLIGHT**: tiny and broken because the batteries inside are covered in the same mysterious sticky filth as the CDs— although how the filth got on the batteries is beyond you

17. **EMPTY CRUSHED JUICE BOX**: under second-row captain's seat

18. **ART PROJECT IN A JAR**: with stickers, sparkles and leaky goo . . . (filth mystery solved)

19. **EMERGENCY BAG**: complete with everything you need for one six-month-old baby. You now have three children. Your youngest is eight years old.

20. **RAISINS**: lots and lots of old, dusty raisins

21. **CHEERIOS**: found only in hard-to-reach places because, for some reason, a dirty Cheerio is still worth eating, while a raisin on the floor or in between the seats is "tainted"

22. **LIP GLOSS AND MASCARA**: When you don't have makeup on and you need a little glamour pick-me-up, lip gloss and mascara are the go-to tools of the modern MILF.

23. **GUM**: Yes, it's a bad habit, but it's great for freshening breath and keeping little mouths busy.

24. **JUICE BOXES**: Keep a few of these in the car in case of dehydration.

25. **CRAYONS AND PAPER**: originally in a large plastic bag marked "Crayons"—ALWAYS a go-to for long rides. Kids of all ages will enjoy drawing.

26. **DISPOSABLE CAMERA**: You didn't see the pole? Someone backed into you??? Prove it.

Yep, a MILF is always prepared.

beauty and the MILF

> You can take no credit for beauty
> at sixteen. But if you are beautiful
> at sixty, it will be your soul's
> own doing.
>
> —MARIE STOPES

MILFs aren't born. They're made. And God knows it's not easy to get there. There are many hurdles and roadblocks on the path to becoming a MILF, and it's not like nature is on your side. Stretch marks, gravity, chicken nuggets—all of these forces conspire to work against us, each contributing to the wide, roaring river called "motherhood" that we must cross daily in order to maintain our sense of humor, sense of self and an ass that doesn't need its own zip code.

You don't need to be a supermodel to be a MILF. You don't have to be a size two, and your booty doesn't need to defy the laws of gravity. MILFs come in all shapes and sizes. A MILF is defined by her confidence, style and vibrance—not human perfection.

However, motherhood is a dirty job—and it doesn't always leave you smelling so good. It's hard to feel beautiful when you haven't showered in three days and even the dog doesn't want to smell your butt. Finding the time and the energy to pull yourself together is a tough battle . . . uphill . . . both ways. You're working around the clock, cleaning spit-up, chasing loose pets, and digging BIONICLEs out of the toilet. Your kids need you, your husband needs you, co-workers need you and *you* need to find that damn Excedrin bottle before your head explodes.

A woman who cannot be
ugly is not beautiful.

—KARL KRAUS

Yes. Motherhood is dirty (and occasionally painful) indeed. But through it all, MILFs retain something extraordinary that plain old mothers simply don't—sex appeal. Allow me to illustrate: even with one hand clutching a squirming guinea pig and the other fishing around a toilet bowl for a submerged toy, a MILF still exudes a vitality, confidence and beauty that others can't ignore. A MILF always gets the job done, and *that's* sexy.

Now, this doesn't mean that in order to be a MILF, you're

expected to work all day, care for the kids, cart them around, cook for them, feed them, bathe them, clean up after them, put them to bed and *THEN* doll yourself up and perform amazing sexual feats on your partner. Not that there's anything wrong with that. Good for you (and good for your partner) if you have that kind of stamina. I don't. And I don't know a lot of women who do.

Being a MILF is about being able to work and care for kids all day, cart them around, cook for them, feed them, bathe them, clean up after them, put them to bed, and *just* as you've finally collapsed in front of the television in those soft, cozy sweatpants that hug your booty and a scoop-neck T-shirt that suggests a bit more than just the fact you're "with Stupid," *your partner* wants to perform amazing sexual feats on you. (And God love 'em if *they* have the stamina. . . .)

You're one hot piece of ass, even with spaghetti sauce in your hair.

Achieving This *Thing* of Which People Speak . . . This "Sex Appeal"

Here's the deal. We are drawn to youth. This may not be what you want to hear and it doesn't sound fair—but it *is* nature. Think about it. People are organic beings—as organic as if we were bees or flowers. It's our nature to want to reproduce and perpetuate our species. A flower is bright and pretty in order to attract bees who will take its tasty pollen and spread it so that more bright and pretty flowers will grow. Likewise, the nectar and pollen from the flowers give the bees the carbohydrates and protein they need. There's a reason you don't see bees hanging around piles of sticks. There's no action there—nothing they need. It's not that bees have something against sticks. It's just that their instincts tell them that sticks aren't going to help them have more little bees—and what's the use in that? Nature even finds a way to reinforce this behavior (young flower = yum / stick = yuck). When the bees taste the pollen of the bright, pretty flower, it tastes sooooooo goooooood. It's sweet, it's succulent and they want more. (Ever taste a honeysuckle? They're so sweet!) Nature makes the flowers delicious to the bees so they'll keep coming back for more. It's a Pavlovian response. Good behavior (spreading the pollen) makes the flowers grow and is rewarded with tasty goodness. Bad behavior (wasting time on a stick) doesn't help nature with her primary purpose of reproduction and is discouraged by giving them icky bee tongue. Nobody wants icky bee tongue.

The truth simply comes down to the fact that whether you're a human, a bee, a flower, whatever, nothing is really attracted to sticks. Except dogs . . . and even then the sticks get chewed up and spit out.

MILFs are like flowers—not the brightly colored daisies

or poppies that spring up here and there and are gone by the end of the season only to show up a year later in someone else's flower bed. No. MILFs are like rosebushes. Beautiful, elegant, healthy rosebushes that bloom annually around a classic white-picket fence. Sure, there are times when the branches are bare and you only see thorns, but every spring they sprout rich, fragrant, juicy blossoms. And there are always more roses than the year before adorning branches that have changed, grown stronger, and now wrap more snugly around that fence—solidifying its position in the yard. And you're surprised and pleased by how much more beautiful the whole thing is—even if the bush is a year older.

Being a MILF isn't about pretending to be young. We're not. (And thank God!) And it's not about attracting young men. (Who has the time . . . ?) It's about being fresh, vibrant and secure—continuing to always grow and being beautiful even when you're bare and your thorns are showing.

MILF Mantra: MAXIMUM effect with MINIMUM effort.

MILFs Keep It Easy

MILFs spend the energy on the areas that have the most impact for the minimal effort. Eyes, lips . . . showering. Simple things we all can do to feel good about ourselves without driving ourselves crazy. Not quite sure how to get there? Look no further. . . .

A MILF drinks lots of water. First and foremost, a MILF approaches her beauty regimen from the inside out. I know, I know . . . you read this in what . . . like, EVERY issue of *Allure*? There's a reason for it. It's TRUE! You need water to hydrate your skin, to hydrate your body . . . oh . . . and to not be so thirsty you reach for a diet soda. (Soda is a beauty no-no—sugar, chemicals, bad for bones, etc. . . .) Eight glasses of water a day is recommended so glug, glug, glug . . . and stick close to a potty.

A MILF enjoys her food. But you're not in your twenties anymore, and eating the steak frites leaves you with more than just an upset stomach. You gain; you bloat; you feel gross. . . . You just don't feel MILFy. (How often do you want to have sex after a late-night burger and fries . . . ?) Again, you've heard this before, but having a low-fat diet and eating whole grains and plenty of fruits and vegetables help contribute to your health and outer beauty. Now, I'm no nutritionist (and God knows I get real crabby if I don't get my monthly hot fudge sundae) but I know I feel my best when I eat well. And when I eat well for an extended period of time, my hair, my skin and *all* of my body parts that are inclined to make unusual sounds, look and behave a lot better. Consult with your doctor or a nutritionist to help you come up with a plan that helps keep you healthy AND happy.

A MILF makes a point to exercise regularly. Yeah, yeah, can't someone recommend a way to feel good while sitting on your sofa watching TV? Here's the problem with that—if you sit on the sofa all day watching TV, you're just not a MILF. So if you want to be a part of the MILF movement, you've gotta . . . well . . . *MOVE!* Study after study shows that exercise improves mood, aids healing and gets the blood flowing—giving you a healthy, beautiful glow. Here's what it comes down to—just get up off your ass! Go for an hour-long walk. Don't have that kind of time? Make time for a half-hour walk. Punch out five minutes of jumping jacks in your own backyard or pick up your daughter's jump rope and do five minutes. My favorite exercise class ever was a "recess-centered" program I used to take at Radu in New York City. It involved all kinds of games you used to play in elementary school. You forget you're exercising and you have built-in PE companions. Play tag with your kids, run races, go biking, play basketball! Just don't sit on the bleachers, or the sidelines, or on that waterproof blanket you tote around in the back of your SUV. Wear your sneakers to the park and get up off your butt. Here's the naked truth: keeping up with your kids physically will help keep you physically fit—and keep you connected with your kids simultaneously! Now, THAT's MILFy multitasking. (But AGAIN, consult with your doctor before beginning or changing any exercise regimen. And don't forget: **a MILF protects her skin** with sunscreen when running around. Lots and lots of sunscreen. Tans are for teens.)

Taking joy in living is a woman's best cosmetic.

—ROSALIND RUSSELL

A MILF showers (at least occasionally). When my twins were in preschool, we had a parents' night at their school. The teacher went around the room and asked all of the parents, "What do you like to do in your free time?" The other moms and dads said things like tennis, golf, baking and hiking. She got to me and I said, "Shower. In my free time I like to shower." Seems almost too silly to mention, but showering is a major accomplishment for moms—especially new moms. But this is one beauty trick that lots of moms underestimate. When you emerge from the tub or the shower cleansed, your hair is clean, your crevices are fresh and you might even feel like you've lost weight (which, after washing all that grime off of you, you may have actually done . . .). It's one extremely simple thing you can do that will energize you, and just plain make you feel good inside and out.

A MILF knows how to use makeup. This does NOT mean that you can line your lips perfectly while driving seventy miles per hour in the HOV lane. It means that when you DO use makeup, you know how to use it to your best advantage.

As you get older, your skin begins to get dull. You just don't have the same natural radiance you had in your twenties. As a result, ALL of the makeup tricks you carefully honed throughout your teenage years and into your twenties just don't work for your face and skin type anymore.

Do yourself a favor. Indulge in an appointment with a makeup artist. A really great makeup artist. Good salons usually have someone solid on staff. You can always try an upscale department store but they are more interested in selling you a specific product than assessing your particular face. Makeup artists understand color and shapes (that's why they're "artists") and can personalize a makeup routine that works for you day and night. I took a makeup lesson from Daniel McFadden at Prive Salon in Los Angeles. He hand-picked colors that were natural but beautiful with my skin type and listened to what I like. Very natural for daytime. Not too dramatic—but with the option to "take it up a notch" at night. Sure, it cost the equivalent of two days of gymnastics camp, but it was the best investment in my beauty routine I ever made. And it just might be the MILF-over you need.

A MILF invests in great makeup and makeup brushes. MILFs are not teenagers anymore, and while better makeup may cost more, you get better pigmentation, they go on more smoothly and they have better staying power. MILFs like staying power. MILFs also keep brushes clean to help ensure your colors look the way you want.

A MILF avoids looking too "done" by doing her makeup by the light of a window. In a bright, sunny room they can see exactly what they're going to look like on that soccer field. Of course, when getting ready for the evening, they add a bit more eye shadow for intensity but keep the blush very natural. Avoid stripes and too-dark colors that make it look like you scraped your cheek on the carpet. That's not pretty.

A man's face is his autobiography.
A woman's face is her work of fiction.

— OSCAR WILDE

A MILF's Makeup Bag

A MILF knows that mascara, eyeliner, eye shadow and lip gloss can transform any face. That's why these four items are the keystones of her makeup bag. Not only do I keep these essentials in my bag at home; I keep an extra set in my car just in case I end up someplace unexpected where I need to look . . . I don't know . . . "better." Sure, I'm on board with the whole "natural" look, but sometimes I want to look awake or like I made an effort. It makes me feel pretty.

For starters, our lashes lose their lushness. They thin out, fall out and look shorter. You can't bat your lashes if it looks like your eyeballs are "bald as a Ping-Pong ball." Like magic, the simple sweep of a little mascara wand will instantly help you look more awake and "prettier." (I think of it as a tiny fairy godmother for your lashes.) Keep fresh mascara handy. (I say "fresh" because we all let ours sit around for months . . . years . . . and think it's fine. It's not. It's filled with bacteria that you literally put next to your eyeball.) Be sure to replace mascara every three to four months.

Then there's eyeliner. A MILF uses this to fill in her lash line. The fabulous makeup artist McFadden taught me how to do a "tight line," where you take an eye pencil, or an eyeliner brush with gel liner on it, and dot it along the *inside* of your upper lash line (the side that's closest to your eyeball).

When you dot along the actual roots of your lashes, you are filling in the lash line to make it look a bit thicker and richer. Obviously, this takes a lot of care, but filling in your lash line this way looks nice and natural.

A MILF may also use an eyelash curler. These are great for making sleep-deprived eyes look more awake. If you've never used one of these, I suggest you have a professional show you how to use this or you could end up yanking precious lashes from your eye. Ouch! You'll need a really good one, and Shu Uemura has the best.

Want to dress it up a bit? A MILF uses an eye shadow in a natural color to highlight her eyes. I love a liquid eye shadow in a tone just slightly lighter than my skin. You just dot it onto your lid and rub it in (not too hard or your sensitive skin will turn red and it will take an hour to go away). Apply a slightly darker color on the outer crease of your eye to give a little depth and direct the outer edges of your eyes upward. MILFs like things on their body to move upward.

And then there are our lips. See those beautiful, cherub lips on your kids? Plump with color and so juicy you want to squeeze them? Yeah. They're cute. You don't have those anymore. It's just a fact—as we get older, our lips get thinner and blotchier. Lipstick and lip gloss, in natural colors, can help even out lip color. A MILF looks for lipstick in a shade complementary to her skin tone—whether it's pale pink or bright red. If your lipstick color doesn't match your skin tone, you'll look like a blow-up doll. Have no idea what your skin tone is? That's what those nice ladies behind the makeup counters at department stores are for. Don't be shy. Ask for help. And lip liner can also be a great way to help define a blotchy lip line and get a natural, fresh shape. HELPFUL HINT: AVOID lip liner you can see! Whether it's paler than your lip color, or brighter, the only lips ever outlined are a clown's.

You can add a bit of pop to the lipstick with a dot or two of lip gloss in the middle of your lower lip, or just apply lip gloss all over to nude lips to clean up your look. Nothing makes you look "fresher" than clean, poppin' lips (that's a nod to Lil Mama).

A MILF doesn't always have time for foundation, especially when she's running late to school. But foundation can even out skin tone. And a simple mineral powder or loose powder doesn't take a great deal of time to apply—with one quick sweep, a MILF can run out the door. A great makeup artist can help you pick a color that looks great with your skin. It should even out your complexion and disappear. Invest in really good makeup sponges and dampen the sponge a bit to blend it all in. Don't forget your neck for a smoother, more seamless look. Looking like a mime is NOT MILFy. But don't discount the au naturel look, which is very MILFy.

Now, I think blush is one thing a MILF can get away without during the day. But if she's wearing foundation, then she should at least add a hint of a simple, natural bronzer (again, to avoid looking like you're a mime . . .). Just a hint, though, because nobody at the bake sale wants to buy cookies from Cruella De Vil.

---

*Beauty comes as much from
the mind as from the eye.*

—GREY LIVINGSTON

MILF Beauty Essentials

Want to know a MILF's secrets to looking great? Open her bathroom cabinets. (Go on. . . . It's so tempting.) Here's what you'll find. . . .

A straightening iron: To smooth out those stray frizzies. Great for bangs to avoid that rounded "helmet" look. **TIP:** Straightening JUST the under layers adds length to a do. Then you can tease the upper part for volume.

A good hair dryer: Not the crappy kind you've had since high school. Something with power and stamina (MILFs like power and stamina. . . .). You can find a professional-grade one at a beauty supply store and (faint alert) they can cost upward of $75, but it'll last rather than break down every few years. Like I always say: "Buy well, buy once."

Want to be beautiful? Think happy thoughts! Christian Renna, DO, of LifeSpan Medicine says, "Most of the background chatter in our mind is worrying, judging, criticizing, defending and complaining. Catch yourself and create a distraction by redirecting your thoughts toward the things that you are grateful for and optimistic about." You can do that, can't you?

Good shampoo and conditioner: There *is* a big difference in shampoos and how they work on your hair now—especially now that you're over thirty-five. You can talk to your hairstylist about recommendations for your specific hair, but don't skimp when it comes to buying a shampoo and conditioner that will be effective in helping to make your hair shiny, strong and healthy.

A great hairbrush: Believe it or not, a good hairbrush makes a difference. For example, a good round boar's-hair brush will help make smoother hair when you straighten it and will assist with glossier waves when you curl. As with any craft, you need the right tools to get the job done.

Good nail polish: When you get a manicure, use your own polish. That way you can do touch-ups if you need to. Clean nails are all you need to keep your hands looking fresh—unless you have the energy to keep up a manicure and repair chipped polish. (Unfortunately, I don't. . . .) Gorgeous reds on toes are practically a "neutral" for MILFs, but steer clear of neons.

Floss: Fighting plaque and promoting gum health are important to MILFs. Carry floss. You never know when a rogue poppy seed or spinach from your salad will try to take up residence in your bicuspids.

Great face cleanser: As a woman of any age, your skin needs extra care. Pores get larger as we get older. Washing your face every morning and every night helps stop dirt from settling in your pores. Incidentally, that same dirt that gets into the pores stretches them out and makes them even larger. What a dirty catch-22. In short—wash!

Toner: Toner picks out dirt your cleanser doesn't reach and can help tighten skin and shrink pores (which helps keep the dirt out). You don't want to strip your skin of natural oils, but find a toner that cleans and tightens without drying you out.

Moisturizer: The second most important thing you can do to preserve your skin. There's lots of trial and error involved with finding the perfect moisturizer that quenches your skin and doesn't make you break out. But the fact is, a GREAT moisturizer WORKS and is so important to maintaining dewy skin and keeping it healthy!

From the Mouths of MILFs: "At a certain point, lingerie turns from frivolity to 'foundation.'"

—LAURA, LOS ANGELES, CA

If you do only one thing, get a great haircut. A great haircut flatters your face, has a stylish but still classic shape, and will grow in well. It's easy to keep up and is one of the best beauty tips around.

Four Bad Habits That Sap You of MILFiness

Lindsey Tanner, an Associated Press medical writer, suggested that four bad habits combined—smoking, drinking too much (more than two drinks daily for women), inactivity (fewer than two hours of physical activity a week), and poor diet (eating fruits and vegetables fewer than three times a day)—aged people on average by twelve years! Yikes! A MILF wants a long, happy, healthy life, so with that in mind . . .

A MILF avoids smoking. It causes wrinkles, makes skin age, and will—quite simply—kill you. You don't look MILFy when you're dead, no matter how good the mortician.

A MILF avoids excessive drinking. Many moms, myself included, enjoy a glass of wine in the evening. I won't lie, I also love a fresh cucumber gimlet or pomegranate mojito every now and again (. . . and again). This works for me, and my doctor has told me my drinking patterns are fine—for me. But be aware that drinking more than a glass of wine every day or binge drinking (which for women means having three or more drinks in one evening) not only affects your waistline but can make your skin look like crap (broken capillaries, dark spots, dry patches . . .). PLUS, it negatively impacts your heart, your liver and your pancreas. So drink responsibly. A MILF likes a pretty pancreas.

A MILF avoids a sedentary lifestyle. You might be thinking, *Sedentary?? I'm a mom! I haven't been sedentary since I was on bed rest at twenty-six weeks with my twins!* Well, that's great, then. Moving on . . .

A MILF avoids the ol' "cheeseburger-a-day" philosophy. This can be a tough one for a mom. Especially when you're actually faced with cheeseburgers . . . and macaroni and cheese, and chicken nuggets, and pizza . . . every day.

But as I mentioned earlier, talk to your doctor and/or a nutritionist to come up with a healthy plan that makes you feel like you're having your cake and eating it too. After all, a MILF doesn't like to be deprived.

Can you imagine a world without men?
No crime and lots of happy fat women.

— NICOLE HOLLANDER

Every MILF has her own individual arsenal of tips, tricks and tools to make her feel fabulous and look great. But there is one device all MILFs employ and it doesn't cost a thing. You won't find it in her bathroom, under her bed or in her closet. Why? She keeps it on her at all times (even when she's not using it). It's her smile.

Past a certain age . . . it's either
your fanny or your face.

— CATHERINE DENEUVE

CHAPTER EIGHT

MILF chic

THE MILF AND STYLE

> **A girl should be two things:**
> **classy and fabulous.**
>
> —COCO CHANEL

MILFs are stylish and elegant. They are dressed head to toe with comfortable ease, ready for whatever the day may bring, be it lacrosse practice, the market or a business lunch. "Good for them," you say as you eyeball the plain suits, shirts and jeans you've had for years. A lot of us hold on to old clothes because we think, *I'll fit into this again . . . one day.* Or maybe you remember how great it made you look when you bought it . . . before you had kids. Maybe you just think, *I don't need to dress up for anyone. I'm fine the way I am.*

Yes, *you* are. But those clothes you've had since college . . . aren't. They're old. They aren't flattering, and when you wear them, it looks like you have completely given up on life. Giving up is not MILFy. But here's some good news. Looking even better and dressing like a MILF doesn't have to mean "dressing up."

This might come as a surprise, but looking like a MILF can be as simple as wearing a nice clean T-shirt and avoiding mom jeans. "MILF Chic," as I like to call it, is a combination of timeless simplicity, personal flair and child-friendly fabrics (you know, the stuff that's easy to clean, easy to wear, nonflammable . . .). Classic style, ease and a creative attitude toward dressing are what turn a mom into a MILF.

The key to MILF Chic is knowing what looks good on your body. Your body changes forever after you have kids. If you want to look good, you need to be honest with yourself. Really honest. I know you love those old jeans, but if they accentuate your "muffin top" rather than that fabulous ass of yours . . . it's time to ditch them.

It's not easy to know what works for your body type, but there are some simple guidelines for hiding trouble spots that can be helpful when you're trying to find pieces to plump up your wardrobe:

Got Tummy? As a general rule (I say "general" because for every rule there is an exception), A-line dresses are great for this shape. They fit closely where you are the slimmest, and camouflage the areas parts of your body that are more full. Likewise, tops that are fitted around your arms and décolleté, then flounce out at the bottom and don't cling around the midsection, are very mommy-tummy friendly. Skinny jeans can work if they have a lot of stretch and if you pair them with a great tunic! Tunics are VERY tummy friendly—and fantastic for BBQs—you can really "pack it away . . ."

Baby Got Back? Again, A-line dresses work well, as do tailored pants creased down the front to give the illusion of height (which makes you look longer). Avoid front pleats and poufs. Focus on your slimmer sections with tailored tops and slimming shawls that drape down the front and over your midsection. Empire waist—which is a waistline that falls under your boobs and gathers and cascades down—is also flattering for this shape. A tank top under a sweater jacket that hangs longer in front looks great with boot-cut jeans. The boot cut balances out the proportions of your legs.

"Hi Janes"? A girlfriend described this to me as the skin under the arm that jiggles back and forth when you raise your arm to wave hi to your friend Jane across the room. Basically, it's a name for the thicker, flabbier arms you can't believe you have despite the fact that you lift a baby every day. Avoid tank tops or wear them with a great sweater or jacket or poncho. God bless the dolman sleeve . . . and the poncho!

T & A? Wrap tops, wrap dresses and tailored clothing all look great. Anything too boxy and you'll look big all over. Pick out clothes that show off your shape.

Just "T" (A Great Rack)? That's awesome! Boobs have never been bigger! (No pun intended.) Don't hide them behind neck-high T-shirts and sweaters—they'll make your chest look larger—and not necessarily in a good way. Scoop-neck T-shirts and V-necks lengthen your neck and open up that beautiful décolleté. Careful not to dip too low. You don't want your cup to runneth over and spilleth out.

You start out happy that you have no hips or boobs. All of a sudden you get them, and it feels sloppy. Then just when you start liking them, they start drooping.

—CINDY CRAWFORD

Maybe you're thinking, *Who has the time to put this much thought into dressing?* Or perhaps you want to scream out, "You don't understand. I just want to make it out the door with my pants right side out." I do understand. But here's a news flash— when you feel good in what you're wearing, you actually *physically* exude more confidence and feel better about yourself.

MILF DUD ALERT! So many people see a cute shirt, great dress or amazing accessory and say, "I MUST have that!" This is a trap. Just because something looks fabulous on a hanger doesn't mean it will look fabulous on you. It's hard for women to fall in love with something and walk away . . . but as with any relationship, if it doesn't love you back, you should let it go. The only way any piece of clothing will actually maintain its fabulousness—from hanger to person—is if it makes *YOU* look better. Otherwise, you might as well take a beautiful painting, put some string around the top of it and wear it as a halter top. It's the same concept—you're just the billboard. Sure, it's a pretty picture, but do you look good with that thing hanging around your neck? Not likely. Not even if you're Heidi Klum.

MILF Mantra: Wear your clothes; don't let them wear you.

TIP: Don't shop alone. Take a friend shopping with you—someone you trust. Someone who will say that makes your arms look thick, your butt look fat, or your boobs look too big. (It's possible, you know—MILFs like to be proportionate.) Of course, this person should also be able to say, "You look like a rail!" "That's so pretty with your skin!" and "You are *gorgeous* in that!" We don't want to shop with Negative Nellys. They're toxic.

Achieving MILF Chic

A MILF wears child-friendly fabrics. Look in any MILF's closet and you find cotton, wool and maybe even bamboo. Sure, you'll spot some silk and perhaps a few other delicate fabrics in there—but she will not be wearing those to the playground. MILFs avoid angora, linen and chinchilla. (Chinchilla is not kid-friendly . . . unless it's alive.)

A MILF makes over her wardrobe. A MILF goes through her closet, takes out everything she hasn't worn in two years and donates it to Goodwill or the school garage sale. I have super stylish MILF friends who insist on the six-month policy . . . but I'm not that strict. I think if you haven't worn it in two years, chances are you're not going to start now.

A MILF plans ahead. A MILF puts aside one night a week or even one night a month and pulls out outfits. She does it at night or when the kids aren't home so she's not in "just throw something on, goddammit!" mode. She thinks about new ways to pair stuff. Maybe she even does it with a girlfriend over a glass of wine. A fresh perspective can bring new life to any mom's wardrobe.

A MILF buys clothes that fit. Moms are all guilty of not purchasing new clothes because we're convinced we can shave off those five or ten extra pounds and get back into our old "reliables." I hate to be the one to break this to you, but they're not reliable at all. In fact, they betray you. They don't fit on your figure anymore, and rather than looking cute, you just look like you're trying to capture "cute." The result? You have a closet full of "nothing to wear." Certainly nothing that makes you feel great. A MILF has some great pieces in her wardrobe that make her feel good! Even if you're convinced you're going to lose that weight, spend a little money and buy at LEAST two pairs of jeans and a few shirts that make you feel fantastic. Have a little extra to spend? Get a great black dress too. Don't want to spend any money at all? Have a few stylish friends who feel the same way? Arrange a clothing swap. It's important to embrace the size you are, or you just won't be able to feel very MILFy. Now, THAT's something you can rely on.

A MILF accessorizes. Want to make a good outfit instantly look great? Add a fabulous accessory. Shoes and bags are a MILF's little "sumpin' sumpin'." You are instantly stylish once you dress up a T-shirt and jeans with gorgeous little flats and a beautiful handbag.

A MILF shows off her jewelry. A MILF doesn't drip in diamonds for a trip to the mall, but a sparkle here and a twinkle there can really brighten up a boring outfit. You have finally earned the right to wear all the good stuff you've acquired so far in your life (engagement ring upgrades, push presents, birthday and anniversary pieces . . .). That four-carat sapphire ring you inherited from your grandmother? That gold bead necklace from the forties your mother let you have? Go ahead—enjoy wearing it to a party or for a night out. Significant jewelry is tacky on young women. You're a grown woman. Enjoy the rewards!

While a MILF accepts her imperfections and accentuates her positives with clothes and accessories that flatter her best attributes, a MILF Dud flaunts her negatives—either because she doesn't see herself as "worthy" or because she is in a deep state of denial. You don't need any help spotting a MILF Dud; you'll see her coming a mile away:

A MILF Dud dresses like she's still in her twenties (when she is . . . ahem . . . not in her twenties): in an effort to appear "hip," she buys into trends whether they flatter her or not; she won't wear anything in a size larger than she was in college—even when she's not the size she was in college; she bares her midriff (and I don't mean in a bikini); she wears colors she likes rather than colors that look good on her; she dresses head to toe in prints; she wears insanely uncomfortable shoes all day long (or, just as bad, wears orthopedic shoes all day long—tsk, tsk); or she dresses to match her children.

MILFs don't let other MILFs turn into MILF Duds.

Dramatic art in her opinion is knowing how to fill a sweater.

—BETTE DAVIS, ABOUT JAYNE MANSFIELD

MILF Wardrobe Essentials

Having the right tools available can help make looking like a MILF as easy as being a MILF. A MILF's wardrobe includes:

T-shirts: MILFs live in these and you need lots of them. MILFs wear them with jeans, nice pants, skirts, layered with others and under sweaters. You'll need them in short sleeves, long sleeves, mid-sleeves and no sleeves (that's a tank top). You'll go through these like tissues. You wear them for five minutes before they're defaced by chocolate milk, syrup or glue. Keep fresh, never-before-worn ones in your closet at all times because inevitably, if you have small children, you'll need to change your shirt before going out in public.

Cover-ups: Shawls, sweaters, cardigans, scarfs, cute jackets that nip in at the waist—each mask and hide the dirty evidence of a MILF's domestic existence. They help make us presentable to strangers and, with the minimum effort possible, make it look like we put a lot of time and care into our appearance. How hard is it to throw on a sweater? The key is LAYERS! Sticky jelly fingers grab you? Your son uses you for a post-pizza napkin? Get puked on? Just peel a layer off! Ta-da! Fresh and clean.

Great black patent leather pumps: The shine is fresh and always a bit more edgy than matte black pumps. They make any outfit look a little more slick, a little more fresh and a little more fun.

A pair of heels in a bright color: Red, pink, orange, green—any bright shade can add pop to any simple, elegant outfit. It injects a tiny bit of humor and personal flair into a simple, classic outfit that could otherwise be less than exciting.

A great pashmina scarf in a bright, flattering color: You should invest in a bright pashmina scarf for the same reason you'll invest in bright heels—they enhance an outfit. It looks SO cute with a nice black leather jacket, T-shirt and jeans. And equally important, it's SO easy to wear and keeps your neck warm and toasty.

A black leather jacket—not the biker kind: Something more tailored and preferably nipped around the waist. It adds a bit of edge to your wardrobe but is also classic.

Jeans: How can we talk about MILFs and not talk about jeans? Buying jeans was my favorite thing to do when I was younger. But now, as I navigate the ever-shifting parabolas of my midsection, it's more complicated. Jeans MUST be flattering. Never too tight and never too loose and NEVER with too much going on—rips, bleaching, studs. Severe acid wash is for the twenty-and-under set. Jeans should flatter your figure and disappear. People should see the MILF, not what the MILF is wearing. The boot cut is the most flattering style for the most body types. Avoid skinny jeans if your midsection is wider and/or going to be exposed.

Two fabulous handbags: One for spring/summer and one for fall/winter. Preferably one in tan or brown and the other black.

GREAT underwear! Every MILF needs to invest in great underwear. Comfortable underwear that doesn't show seams and bras that fit! Go to a department store or a lingerie store and get fitted. It's worth it! A great silhouette is only achieved with great underwear.

> *traditional underpants*—cover completely in the front and in back. These come in seamless options that hide panty lines fairly well. Good if you feel most comfortable with standard coverage.

boy shorts—These are full underpants, but the leg openings fall a bit lower at the top of the thigh. The concept behind these is that you have full underwear but don't get those nasty panty lines because the seams fall below the butt. These are great with skirts or dresses so you have a smooth line, but don't have an overexposed bottom if the wind catches your skirt.

thong—covers completely in front but minimally in back. My kids call this "butt-crack underwear." But the lack of a full back means no panty lines when I'm wearing pants or shorts.

G-string—otherwise known as "butt floss." These are teeny, tiny thong-like undies that have virtually no coverage at all, with the exception of a triangle of fabric in front. I personally don't think they serve any real purpose—other than to just be all hot-cha-cha. But I have a few friends who swear by them. To each her own.

"commando"—the no-underwear option. Personally, as a brunette, I don't endorse commando, and if you're a brunette too, you know why. If you're not, think about what happens when you put a black bra under a light T-shirt. You see my point. But there are lots of women out there (people I share meals with) who love to go commando. Sure, you save on buying underwear, but you have to wash your clothes ALL of the time! That just seems like a lot of laundry to me.

At least three great bras: Get fitted at a lingerie store or a department store (the higher-tier stores usually provide fittings). A good bra makes for a smoother look (front and back) and helps your boobs look great. Never underestimate the importance of great boobs. A MILF has at least two in nude with straps, and one in nude that is strapless. Want to expand your lingerie wardrobe? Think black. WARNING: Bright colors and frilly bras can show under your clothes.

SPANX! Because sometimes good underwear isn't enough. They squeeze you in, tuck you down and hold you up. They're genius! And an absolute necessity for feeling fabulous.

Lovely female shapes are terrible complicators of the difficulties and dangers of this earthly life, especially for their owner.

—GEORGE DU MAURIER

Still confused about fashion? Still skeptical about style? Still wondering how (or even why) you'd be up all night with a screaming baby and still care enough the next day to try to match your T-shirt to your shorts? Here's a very simple rule of

MILF Chic even the most sleep-deprived, totally exhausted, completely worn-out MILFs can follow: *Love your body* (After all, it's done some pretty awesome stuff), love yourself (You deserve it!), and wear what makes you feel good (even if it goes against *all* of the rules above). When you feel fabulous, it shows from the inside out, and feeling great is ALWAYS in style!

CHAPTER NINE

MILF
and
cookies

THE MILF AND MOTHERHOOD

> Giving birth is little more than a set of muscular contractions granting passage of a child.
> Then the mother is born.
>
> —ERMA BOMBECK

A woman becomes a mother when her first child is born. She's the end result of a nine-month-long struggle for supremacy, culminating in a messy battle of body and baby that results in two wholly unique and separate people—a mother and a baby. It's only when that mother refuses to let "the woman she was" be expelled from her body with the afterbirth that she becomes something so much more—a MILF.

A MILF knows who she is, what she wants and how to get it—she's alive. And there is nothing sexier than a woman who's *alive*. (And I don't mean "breathing." Yes, breathing can be very sexy, but it should always be accompanied by some other tantalizing activity.)

Ironically, and quite contrary to this purpose, motherhood

is the most all-consuming job a woman can have, and leaves little if no time at all to think about yourself. It's easy to forget how much you need a shower when you have a child or two (or, God help you, more . . .) who want your undivided attention with unwavering priority, be it for a major school report or for wiping a runny nose.

You can give everything you have, every minute, every hour, *every* fiber of your being to these little people, but they will never willingly give you five minutes of solitude to poop. And when you spend all of your time with a group of short, demanding people who never see you as an individual, it's easy to lose sight of yourself. That's the irony of motherhood . . . and Hollywood . . . but motherhood too.

My point is, if you don't make time for your own happiness—to nurture your individuality, your brain and your sexuality—you *will* wake up one day, look in the mirror and say, "Mom??!! What are you doing there??" No one wants that. Especially your husband.

What Happened?
Where Did She Go?

One day you're a carefree spirit, having sex with your husband at one a.m. in the guest bathroom at a friend's cocktail party, and the next you're scarfing down dessert because you have to be home by ten p.m. to relieve the babysitter. There was once a time when you always had it together. You could do it all. Work, play and maintain a sex life. Your hair was always clean, your clothes matched, you spoke in complete sentences and the word "pull-ups" meant you had a good workout. You had luxurious phone conversations with friends that would go on for hours, and you knew what was happening in the world. Yes. You were childless.

Sound like a faint memory?

From the moment you started accepting congratulatory calls in the recovery room, all that changed. Simply remembering which nipple you last used for nursing became an enormous task. Once you had children, your goals were reduced to buying everything you needed at the market in one shot.

But you can be efficient again! A MILF is just such a multitasking machine that she needs to implement a few strategies to ensure she gets her kids to soccer and still doesn't forget about the class bake sale. A MILF uses lists and schedules to create calm out of chaos. She seeks out shortcuts, implements useful tools and finds intuitive reminders to help maintain a sense of order . . . and keep her sanity.

With the help of some MILFs who've "been there, done that," I've pulled together some tips, advice and strategies to help you on your way to total MILFdom. You too can manage car pools, sibling rivalry, puke-stained sweaters and children who scream in public (in short . . . motherhood), and still be one red-hot momma!

MILF Mantra: Sanity equals beauty.

Ever see a beautiful, confident, pulled-together woman in an asylum? Nope. Know why? Nothing makes you look crappier than insanity. Organizing your life and getting it under control is the best way to ensure a serene facade. A MILF knows this (and fears it a little), and does her best to arrange and systematize her life so she can handle the insanity without feeling like she needs a straitjacket:

A MILF has her kids lay out their clothes the night before. This prevents morning dillydallying and the inevitable whines of "I have nothing to weaaaaarrrrrr!" and "MAAAAAA???? Where are my socks?" or "Moooooom???? I have no pants!!!!" when a MILF has only five minutes to make it to school before the bell. If everything the kids need to be fully dressed is out and waiting for them in the morning, all they have to do is put it on. Of course, you can only lead a horse to water. . . .

A MILF lays out her own clothes the night before. Not only does this take the morning pressure of "What shall I wear?" off your shoulders, but if a MILF uses this tactic wisely, she could get a good five, ten, maybe even fifteen minutes of extra sleep out of her morning! Imagine just hitting the alarm and rolling out of bed and right into the clothes you laid out. A MILF will look way better on the days she plans than on those when she's reached for clothing with half-closed eyes and a sleepy mind. This also prevents wearing two different shoes. (Yes . . . I've done this.)

A MILF makes lunches the night before. Right about now you're probably thinking, *What the hell?! When do I get to enjoy my evenings! Forget this MILF sh*t and hand me a glass of wine and the remote!* It may sound like I'm suggesting a MILF spend her entire evening prepping for her mornings. But here's the thing . . . once you figure out a system that works for you—and you have it down pat—you'll find you not only have an easier morning rush, but your downtime in the evening is more relaxing because you don't have to worry about the morning stampede to get out the door. Got older kids? A MILF knows she can have them help make their own lunches. Just don't let them forget to grab their lunches as they run out the door.

A MILF makes dinner in advance—hours or even days before it gets served. You know how it goes—once you pick up the kids from school and take them from karate to dance and then to Mandarin lessons, your afternoon and early evening are completely shot. A working MILF uses that peaceful time after kids have gone to sleep or when the older ones are doing homework or watching TV as a chance to pull together what she'll need for meals the next day or even for that week. Knowing you have something in the fridge you can just pop into the microwave or oven will make your evenings significantly less crazy and can help make your "family time" more about "family" than stirring risotto (which I don't recommend as a family dinner—SOOOO time consuming!)

A MILF uses her kids! No, not to get out of a speeding ticket. Once you have kids big enough to tackle chores, you can use them to take out the trash, set the table, clean out the hamster cage, put away their own laundry, bring in groceries, even make their own snacks so you're not "on call" every time they get the munchies. Now, obviously they can't wash the windows on the second floor, but give them a task that you feel they're ready to handle. Even little ones can sort dirty laundry into darks and lights. A MILF figures that if you're all one big family, then everyone should pitch in. Of course, it's a bonus that chores teach kids responsibility *and* help lighten Mom's load.

A MILF keeps a to-do list and looks at it every day. Do you spend the day running errands only to have completely forgotten the cable guy was coming? Do you work all day only to get home and realize you forgot your son's school has a bake sale the next day and you're in charge of four dozen brownies? I'll share another theory. Our minds are like stick-on bras. The older we get, the more stickiness we lose. When we're fresh and new, everything can be held together in one place. But perhaps we should take note of the aging bra that loses its hold and after a while just slips and a boob pops out. Don't be that boob. Use the to-do list app on your phone or computer and look at it EVERY morning! If you don't use a PDA, write a list and keep it on your fridge. A dry-erase board is a great tool.

A MILF teaches the kids to stick closely to a schedule. When kids know where they're supposed to be and what they're supposed to be doing, they move more quickly and balk less. At the beginning of every week print out a copy of your calendar from your computer (after it's been synced with your PDA, please!). Highlight each kid's activities in a different color and hang the schedule on the fridge. Still in the twentieth century? Keep a monthly dry-erase board calendar in your kitchen. Write out everyone's activities for the month using a different color of dry-erase marker for each member of the family (including yourself).

Even if your little ones can't read, they can tell they have something to do (a chore, a playdate, a class . . .) just by seeing their color. Like grown-ups, they'll believe anything they see in writing.

A MILF talks to mom friends. Venting aids sanity. Talk to your friends and swap stories. The good and the bad! Sharing the motherhood experiences with other MILFs will feel great and help keep you from feeling like you're crazy. (More on this in Chapter 12: The "MILF's MILF": The MILF and Friendship.)

A MILF has a reliable babysitter. Preferably once or twice a week, but at the absolute least once every other week! A MILF will go to dinner, go to a movie, go to a comedy club, play pool, go bowling, grab a cocktail with a friend—she'll go wherever and not talk about kids! You can't be a MILF if you don't have the time to remember what a MILF you are. A MILF needs to get out with grown-ups, without children, so she can have adult conversations and connect with other grown-ups on her own level. Every now and again, preferably on a regular basis, a MILF will just put her kids in capable hands and go out and have a good time. MILFs love their families, but they also need to let loose and have fun.

*The quickest way for a parent
to get a child's attention is to sit
down and look comfortable.*

—LANE OLINGHOUSE

A MILF makes herself a priority. If you don't, who will? Not all the time, but at least once every day, a MILF remembers to take at least a little bit of time for herself. Even if it's just five minutes to let your morning coffee sink in. And she is a better mother and all the more beautiful for it!

A MILF will nap. Studies have shown that a short nap (fifteen to twenty minutes is suggested for best results) in the middle of the day can energize you. Why do you think European women always look so fresh? Siestas! It feels *sooooooooooo* good. MILFs like to feel good. And honestly, this may be one of the hardest goals on the list to achieve, but if you can, oh, wow, do you deserve a MILF honorable mention!

A MILF says "no" and MEANS IT! Nothing sucks the life out of a mom like saying, "No. No. No. No. No . . ."

a thousand times. You wonder, *Am I speaking a foreign language?* Well, if you're the kind of mom who makes a habit of saying "no" and *THEN* caves in and says "yes" five minutes later . . . then you *ARE* speaking a foreign language—and it's called "Wishy-Wash-ese." To your kids, "no" actually means, "I don't want to let you but my tolerance is running really thin right now because I hate this traffic and I still have no idea what I'm going to make for dinner and if you keep going, I might just kill myself . . . or you . . . so please stop asking, stop asking, stop asking. . . . I can't take it anymore. . . . Okay, FINE!" Well, that's not "no" at all. If you are going to say "no" to your kids, whether it's about staying up late, eating candy, going on a playdate or tossing their broccoli to the family dog, MEAN IT! Kids will learn you say what you mean and there will be a LOT less of the "Please, please please . . . !" that can drive any mom insane.

A MILF will have a glass of wine. I don't endorse drinking before car pool, but a glass of wine at the end of the day every now and then can be a lovely and MILFy indulgence. Worried about drinking too much and slurring the words to "Hush, Little Baby"? Here's a good MILF rule. . . . Never drink alcohol to quench your thirst. Who hasn't sucked down a glass of wine because you're just so damn thirsty and it's the only beverage within arm's reach? Next thing you know, you're hiccupping and swaying through bath time. No one wants your kids to grow up, walk past some wino on the street and have the realization, *That's funny, something smells like Mom. . . . Hey, wait a minute . . . !* A MILF will have a glass of water first and then enjoy her wine at a more luxurious pace.

A MILF exercises. Exercise is extremely important to being a MILF. Not only do studies show that regular exercise decreases the rate of aging, improves mood and gives people more energy, but it helps to clear your head, keeps you in tune with your body and makes you feel just plain better about yourself. Regular exercise will help you feel in control. So go ahead and clear your mind and make yourself feel good. MILFs like to feel good.

A MILF schedules time every day to be alone with each child. Moms spend all day juggling not just their kids' schedules, but also their kids' attention. Multiple kids make it impossible to give anyone undivided attention. The remedy? Make time every day to be alone with each child. Even if it's only fifteen minutes at bedtime. A MILF will ask her kid about his day. Ask who he played with. Ask him what was good about his day. Or what was bad. Have teenagers who refuse to share even the minutest bit of personal information? A MILF will play a game with her teen: Scrabble, poker, anything! MILFs take the time to get to know their kids. Giving a child undivided attention on a regular basis lets a mom really connect to who she is and makes every child feel good.

idea for "mommy and me" time

If you're anything like me, playing Barbies can put you to sleep. I've been known to specifically request being "the baby" for a game of "house" just so I can nap. But *have dinner alone with one child each week*. One MILF I know with two sets of twins passed along this idea to me. (You heard me . . . *two* sets of twins.) She is a working MILF with long hours, but she sets aside one night every week to take one of her kids out to dinner and they have a night out alone. The Mommy and Me time has been invaluable to her—connecting her to each of her children on a regular basis for a significant chunk of time. It's precious time for her kids, who love having her attention all to themselves.

A MILF cultivates "me" time. Everyone needs it, everyone wants it, but a MILF makes it happen! If you don't make the time, no one's going to hand it to you on a silver plate. ("Here, Mom, have some extra time. . . .")

A MILF gets a hobby! I can't emphasize this enough. MILFs need to expand their minds and fuel the "woman" inside "the mom"! Whether you work "in" or "out" of the home, just trying something novel (or maybe actually starting a novel) can spark new life in your daily routine and amp up your energy level. Photography, cooking, wine tasting, improvisation, pottery, gardening, joining a book club, jewelry making, taking art history classes or writing classes, ANYTHING that gets your mind to think in new ways and feeds your intellect. MILFs have huge intellects, and like huge intellects in others.

A MILF laughs! Taking a step back from that kid who just spilled cereal on the floor to watch them pick it up piece by piece—then eat it—is actually funny. Laughter relieves stress. Not everything is quite as bad as it seems to be in the moment. Find the funny, and like I say on my website, Mommy Lite Online, "Lite'N Up!"

*My mother's menu consisted of two
choices: take it or leave it.*

—BUDDY HACKETT

**A MILF doesn't live with piles; when in doubt,
throw it out!** MILFs don't like to live among piles of broken toys, cheap (and already forgotten) party favors, past
school projects, too-small clothing, worn-out shoes and old
Halloween candy. It makes us feel dirty and bogged down.
Throw stuff out that you don't need, use or want! This doesn't
have to apply to the MILF container, though, as perfection
isn't achievable.

**A MILF doesn't run errands on her own time that
she can run with her kids.** It seems like a no-brainer to
go to the market when you don't have kids with you begging
for cookies and Cocoa Puffs. But this is *your* time! Whether
you work full-time or you're a stay-at-home mom, the time
when the kids are at school is the best time to work, exercise,
get your hair colored, get a bikini wax, anything you would do
more effectively and enjoyably with a little peace and quiet.
Don't have any choice but to bring the brood, but don't want
to listen to them bitch and moan from the produce to the

pasta aisle? Find little "jobs" for them: pointing out supermarket specials by their bright little tags, finding a certain shaped pasta, counting oranges. It'll help kick them into "I wanna do it!" mode.

A MILF doesn't overcommit. MILFs are good people. *You're* good people. That's one of the reasons you're in such high demand. But you don't have to sign up for every volunteer position on the block to prove it. PTA, Girl Scouts, Boy Scouts, charities, classroom volunteer—all of these are admirable causes. But if you overcommit, you won't do any of them very well. Plus, you'll feel angry and put out. Pick what's most important to you and put your best foot forward. Don't be afraid to decline a job if you can't make it work. You don't need to make excuses. After all, "no" is a complete sentence.

---

*Biology is the least of what
makes someone a mother.*

—OPRAH WINFREY

A MILF doesn't carpool. I know, I know . . . this sounds crazy. Carpooling makes life EASIER—right? Yes . . . sometimes it does. But it also takes a lot of planning and you have to rely on other people. When people can't do what they promise to do, the last-minute juggling can push any mom over the edge. You end up putting your sanity in someone else's hands. PLUS you could potentially end up with a brat or two in your car—and they're not even your own. Do *you* want that? I don't think so. If you get asked to carpool and it feels like it could get complicated, or you just think their kid is a pain in the ass, just say no.

We spend the first twelve months of our
children's lives teaching them to walk
and talk and the next twelve telling
them to sit down and shut up.

—PHYLLIS DILLER

A MILF isn't stupid. MILFs hate stupid people. Why? Stupidity is a time suck. You know what I'm talking about. We all do stupid things: leave the house without your wallet, forget to pick up a kid for car pool, forget where your keys are even though you just had them in your hands five seconds ago . . . As moms we tend to drift into autopilot. Believe me, I get it. Being half-conscious allows us to think about more than one thing at once. However, running on autopilot can also derail you and cost you time, and is the perfect breeding ground for stupidity. For example, you're getting your kids out the door, just like you do every day: you pack lunch, fill water bottles, put away cereal and milk, pick up keys from the bowl on the counter . . . But then the phone rings unexpectedly and you put down your keys to answer it. You go back to your "routine," get everyone into coats, and when you go to walk out the door you say, "Where the hell are my keys??" You were on autopilot. You didn't even REALIZE you were putting down your keys. Now, if you could just FOCUS when you put down the keys to answer the phone, OR made a point of never putting down the keys unless it was on their designated hook—you wouldn't be late to school because you were looking for keys. In short? We would all save lots of time if we could *just* stop doing stupid things.

A MILF isn't too hard on herself. Because we *just* can't stop doing stupid things. It's our nature as human beings. (Breathe, eat chicken, be stupid . . .) And moms have it the worst. Multiple kids, multiple schedules, multiple demands on your time—DON'T beat yourself up. MILFs know they're not perfect. Imperfection is hot.

A MILF may accomplish a couple of these most of the time or most of these some of the time, but she's always at work to keep things moving along as smoothly as possible. In the meanwhile, in her spare (I'm sorry. . . . I need a moment to squelch a laugh . . .) time, a MILF dreams that one day SOMEONE will invent these devices to make her life all the more manageable (Is it too much to dream?):

The iMom—keeps multiple schedules for multiple kids in corresponding colors; sends alerts with different sounds for each child's activities; keeps track of all of your kids' current clothing and shoe sizes and makes precise projections of growth based on past growth patterns; tells you what's fresh in your fridge at that very moment; keeps you up-to-date on your kids' immunizations; and has a button you can press that says, "No," so you can save your voice.

The Bloodhound—locates anything that goes missing (within a fifty-mile radius). When you upload an image or give a verbal description of what is missing, it sends out a signal to detect that device/item/piece of jewelry/favorite lipstick and uses a beep that plays "hot and cold" with you till you find it.

The washing machine with pocket detection—senses if a non-fabric-based item (crayons, wads of old tissues, money, small animals) is in the wash and won't turn on until that item is removed.

The automatic front-car-door opener—senses you need a hand and opens the car door. Sure, it's great the kids can zip into the car in the rain, but you're still stuck trying to juggle your umbrella, handbag and kids' backpacks.

Wii Chores—It's not right that your kid can disarm a nuclear warhead using only a nunchuck and his right thumb, but has no idea how to maneuver a vacuum cleaner back and forth. Wii Chores helps your child acquire the skills he needs to clean the house, wash the car and walk the dog.

The Tampon Warmer—just because this was suggested to me once and I thought, *Wow . . . that would be nice.*

Here's what you need to remember: motherhood is the most challenging job you'll ever have, but unfortunately, no one has invented a formula for success. Why? Families are made up of different people, with different needs and different ways of doing things. How could there possibly be one right way to do it all! But here's the good news: a MILF never believes for a minute that being a great mom means being perfect. So pick your battles, forgive yourself for being twenty minutes late to soccer practice, and if you see an outstretched helping hand, go ahead and grab it. Just use a little hand sanitizer first.

the MILF
and marriage

No matter how happily a woman
may be married, it always pleases
her to discover that there is a
nice man who wishes that she
were not.

—H. L. MENCKEN

Marriage changes a woman forever.

It's a slow mutation that typically takes place over six
months to a year, as the course of an engagement is played
out, wedding plans are made and the diamond ring that
marks you as "taken" magically transforms you in the eyes of
those around you from single girl to married woman. Toaster
ovens, guest towels and glassware are the bricks that pave the
road leading from one existence to the other—the material
choices that will serve as the stage of your future.

The first thing you do when you get engaged, after calling
every person you've ever met, is register. China, crystal, silverware . . . all of the household imperatives that will ensure
your future Thanksgivings are a success. In your imagina-
tion you see small, clean children of varying sizes wearing

matching velvet dresses and knickers, sitting politely at the perfectly decorated table while you—their glorious mother—primped and dressed in some beautifully detailed new outfit, emerge from the kitchen carrying a twenty-five-pound golden brown turkey. Your entire brood cheers. They LOVE turkey! What a perfect day.

Thank goodness you have that china.

You cling to this image as tightly as you do your bouquet as you march down the aisle toward that handsome man at the altar. You vow to be each other's number one priority forever and to always make time for sex.

Then you have kids, and the whole thing is smashed to pieces—your priorities, the sex and, especially, the china.

Transitioning from wife to mother changes you and your marriage as profoundly as saying, "I do." Only this transition doesn't occur over an extended period of time. It's instantaneous. One moment, you're a PYT (That's a "pretty young thing," for those of you who missed the eighties), with a husband, a complete set of china and an awesome sex life. The next, you're a mom . . . sex-deprived, exhausted and using mismatched plasticware with princesses and dump trucks on it. Oh, and who's the husband?!

Taking care of kids, maintaining your relationship with your husband, finding time for sex—hell, feeling sexy at all—all become monumental feats. How can you even *think* about sex when your kid's report on life in a coral reef is due the next day and you still haven't found a shoe box big enough for the diorama?

It's a wonder you even manage to find time to eat. But with a little motivation, a little planning and a few good ideas to get you jump-started, you can get in touch with your inner MILF and—if you're lucky—your husband can too.

MILF Mantra: Feed the couple; fuel the family.

A MILF understands that she and her spouse are the backbone of the family unit. When a MILF and her man feel strong and connected, when they're communicating and in sync, family life runs more smoothly and is more enjoyable for every member of the family.

A MILF will send her man love notes. A MILF doesn't need a birthday, an anniversary or a week apart to have a reason to write her honey a letter. She'll often just write a little note that says, "You looked really cute when you came out of the shower today—I wanted to jump you!" It makes him feel good—and reminds you of how cute he is.

A MILF will plan date night at least twice a month—whether it's dinner, a movie, drinks and appetizers or time together without the kids at a coffee shop. A MILF makes it a point to get out of the house *without the kids* and enjoy being with her husband. She knows it's important to make time to connect with her partner regularly.

I don't understand why Cupid was chosen to represent Valentine's Day. When I think about romance, the last thing on my mind is a short, chubby toddler coming at me with a weapon.

—AUTHOR UNKNOWN

A MILF will arrange sleepovers for all of her kids because she's eager to have quality time at home with her husband. She'll employ local grandparents or really good family friends just so she can get back in touch with that couple who would stay up late talking and getting to know each other.

A MILF will e-mail her husband regularly during the day, detailing what bills she's paid, the errands that she needs done, and who he needs to pick up from where.

There is WAY less confusion this way and she gets the help she needs because he is always on e-mail (no excuses). This MILF isn't all business, though; she'll send her husband a sweet e-mail. Or sometimes a sexy e-mail.

A MILF will engage in iSex from time to time. She texts her man, in great detail, the exact things she'd prefer to be doing with him at the very moment they are apart. Out with the girls for the night? Text your man during dinner and you'll end your evening with a bang.

A MILF will have sex BEFORE she goes out! This is my favorite bit of advice from a MILF friend and something I hadn't even considered! Yes! Sex *before* I'm exhausted and bloated like an orca from an evening's meal of pasta and ice cream sundaes (my standard Saturday-night fare). Have the babysitter arrive a few minutes early and sneak away with your man. It puts you in a good mood for the evening and sends you out for the night feeling more "connected."

A MILF will ask for help. A MILF knows her husband isn't a mind reader. If she feels like she's drowning and needs help, she'll ask for it. A MILF isn't afraid to speak up for what she needs. Not speaking your mind only leads to resentment. Resentment is unMILFy.

A MILF asks for what she wants! Again . . . because your husband isn't a mind reader. You want more sex? You want flowers? You want to take a trip to Italy just the two of you one day? Don't hold it against him that he doesn't know. SAY something! A MILF speaks her mind to get what she wants and what she needs. Like I said, resentment is unMILFy.

A MILF will make a dish she knows he likes, because she knows it will make him feel special. No, it's not the 1960s and you don't need to put a bow in your hair. But something simple like making a meal your husband likes reminds him you care. Men are like babies: they need to see physical signs of your affection. Then let him thank you—if he's like James Ingram, he'll find one hundred ways.

A MILF enjoys touching her man. She'll offer foot rubs or massages. Of course, these work both ways, but just having your hands on the person you love can make you feel a bit "spicy." Unless his feet smell. Then a back rub is fine. Or maybe she'll brush his hair and have him brush hers. . . . Remember sitting around at sleepaway camp and you and your girlfriends would brush one another's hair? Ahhhhhhh!! It feels awesome! And you don't need to be a genius with your hands to do it well.

A MILF will take mini-trips with her man. A MILF will try to get away with her husband for a weekend. She may not go far. She may even stay at a local hotel if she can't leave town. Having a hotel room is a great aphrodisiac.

A MILF will have oral sex. Give it. Get it. Do what you like and do it often. Nothing is sexier than someone who clearly enjoys her partner's body. MILFs aren't slutty—not outside their own bedroom, at least—but they are "enthusiastic."

A MILF will just do IT! Exhausted? Crabby? Just not feeling "amorous"? Every now and then, a MILF just goes ahead and has sex anyway. Even if she's not in the mood. Chances are she'll be glad she did.

The simple truth is, marriage is work. Hard work! And it's even tougher once you have kids! But a MILF cherishes her marriage and does what she needs to do in order to nourish and preserve it, whether it's taking the time to say "thank you" to your partner, asking for help when you need it, or just being able to sit back and enjoy the many rewards of married bliss (just don't forget to lock the door).

(CHAPTER ELEVEN)

a single serving of MILF

> The most remarkable thing about my mother is that for thirty years she served the family nothing but leftovers. The original meal has never been found.
>
> —CALVIN TRILLIN

Life is different for a single mom.

The general belief seems to be that if you're a single mom (whether by "choice" or divorce or widowhood), you're a cougar. You're up for boozing and boys, you hate to be alone, you'll have sex with anyone, and you're constantly on the prowl. Women hide their husbands, girlfriends guard their boyfriends, and college boys ogle you like you're an In-N-Out Burger.

It's unfair.

But single moms are people too and not animals that need to be tamed. They have friends, love their children (and don't ditch them at every opportunity), pay their bills on time, and are not psychotic (unless we have our periods . . . then watch out). They are alive and, most of all, complete. And *that's* what makes a single mom a MILF. After all, a single serving of MILF is a whole carton too.

People sometimes forget that a single mom is a whole parenting unit too. They see a single mother and instinctually view her as incomplete, or missing something, or worse . . . broken—even when this conception is completely unfounded. Why do I say this?

There was a time during my marriage when I didn't wear my wedding ring. It was stupid, really. I got into a fight with my husband (now my ex) and, in full drama mode, I threw my rings at him to teach him a lesson. To teach me a lesson, he kept them. For a year.

During that time I walked around without a wedding band, without an engagement ring, completely "unmarked" as married, and I learned a lesson, all right. But not the lesson my ex had intended. Unmarried women over a certain age are stereotyped, and it's not fair.

Obviously, my friends were unmoved by my naked hand. They laughed at my fruitless attempt to get my husband's attention and congratulated him on teaching me the value of a diamond. But the people I met every day—at preschool, at ballet, at the market, out to dinner—were an entirely different story.

I noticed day after day that a lot of women were colder. I'd strike up conversations with random moms at ballet or the bakery with harmless queries like, "How long has your daughter taken ballet?" or "Doesn't that chocolate cream pie look tasty?"—just like I'd always done—but they shut me down. They'd turn their bodies, avoid eye contact, and mumble their answers. "I don't like pie." They clearly didn't want to fully engage. Did I have bad breath? Were they afraid I was a weirdo? (Personally, I don't think commenting on chocolate pie is weird—in fact, I think *not* liking pie is weird.) It just seemed strange to me. After all, ring or not, I was the same pie-lovin' gal I had always been. Without my ring, was I perceived as competition? A prowling cougar who'd plot to take their man if they opened their private world to me by admitting they like pie? Would my "singleness" rub off on them? Was I contagious?

What I hated the most was being treated with pity or like I was "broken." It was obvious I was an "older" woman (i.e. in my mid/late thirties) and if I didn't have a wedding ring, surely something must be wrong with me. I was on par with a creepy drifter you don't want to be rude to but don't want to engage with either. It was like I wasn't "whole" because I wasn't married. Their sideways glances and attempts to politely avoid speaking to me were obvious UNTIL they learned I was actually married (I suppose I kept yapping just long enough to eventually mention my husband)—and *then* their demeanor changed. "What's that? You DO like pie? How interesting . . ."

As for the married men I met, they seemed nervous. Like

they might say the wrong thing. What if I hit on them? How would they handle that? I could practically see the thought bubbles above their heads. We'd exchange pleasantries with simple words like "Hey" or "Could I borrow your salt?" The married man would say, "Yup," and the bubble over his head would type out, "Crap! I think she wants me. What do I do next?! I don't know if I'm ready for this. . . ." It seemed like they thought if they opened the door even a crack, I would jump them right there. You know . . . 'cause I was single.

You doubt me? I was actually at a party with a married girlfriend and we were talking to this really talented, young (and, yes, cute) photographer. He wouldn't even make eye contact with me. Okay . . . maybe he didn't like me. I mean REALLY didn't like me. That's fine. A MILF doesn't need constant adoration to feel fabulous.

So I was ready to walk away and liberate him from my company when I mentioned something about "having to get home to my husband." The photographer did a total 180 and was suddenly chatty. I believe there may have even been some physical contact with my sleeve. Obviously now that I was "safe," he didn't have to worry about me wanting to bear his children. It was gross, and I walked away. He shouted out, "Call me!" (No, he didn't really . . . but that would have been funny.)

I know this sounds crazy. You're probably thinking I'm self-absorbed or being overdramatic—just like when I threw the rings. (This MILF does occasionally get caught up in a little drama.) But I was seriously so surprised by the contrast between how people acted around me when I was "marked" versus "unmarked" that when I eventually got the rings back (I had a twenty-year high school reunion and my ex wanted it to be clear that I was married), I did a little experiment. Some days I wore my rings and some days I didn't—just to see if I was out of my mind. I wasn't. Okay, this *obviously* wasn't a scientifically airtight experiment, but it sure felt like I was experiencing some kind of social phenomenon.

When I eventually got divorced and became single for real (I know what you're thinking: *How could your ex let a ring-throwing, pie-loving girl like you go?!* Yeah, yeah.), I noticed a permanent shift in attitudes toward me from both my male and female married friends. Perhaps friends' husbands were afraid I'd give their wives "ideas," and my female friends didn't seem to need a third or fifth wheel, or seventh wheel . . . whatever. Maybe they thought I'd be uncomfortable. Maybe they were uncomfortable.

So let's set the record straight. I am single and I am happy. Yes, I have a boyfriend. But even when I didn't, I was *still* a happy single mom. On top of that—my kids are happy. Don't get me wrong—they would never admit it. In fact, they're the first to tell me how much their lives suck—but they're doing great. I know, I know . . . it's too much to absorb! "But . . . how can that be? You're over thirty-five . . . and *siiiingle*?!" Yes,

I know. I am. I am single, and I love it. And do you know what? I know lots of other single moms who love it too. They're happy and they're flourishing! They are content with where they are in life, happy with how they look (They DON'T all get fake boobs and face-lifts) and they go through life with a general sense of well-being (unless some asshole driver cuts them off. Turns out, single MILFs are prone to road rage—the result of a lack of access to a dependable, steady stream of sex. But we can't have it all, right?).

Single MILF Mantra: Keep it SIMPLE!

Maintaining the delicate balance of sanity and motherhood can be even trickier for a single mom. So in addition to the dos and don'ts for maintaining maximum MILFiness that you read about in Chapter 9: MILF and Cookies: The MILF and Motherhood, here are the single MILF's dos and don'ts:

A single MILF will Organize! Organize! Organize! Have a professional organizer come to your house for one week, a couple of days, even one day—whatever you can afford. (If you have only one day, make sure you spend your time efficiently by having all of your loose papers filed into folders ahead of time.) Have them help you get your house into peak efficiency mode. Can't afford it? Go to the bookstore or get online and buy a book on organizing your life. Then you can ask a friend to help watch the kids and spend a few hours going through the book. If this still seems ambitious, then just sort through ALL of your papers and create a system you'll USE for keeping receipts, bills, urgent stuff you need to do, and kids' paperwork. MILFs like organization.

A single MILF has a place for everything and everything in its place. I once calculated that I spent a total of two weeks a year just looking for things. If I had only put them away—or created a space where I could put them away—I could have saved myself SO much time. Keep plastic drawers in your utility closets and mark the drawers' contents with a marker or sticker or a Brother P-touch (I love mine!). And when you're done with something, PUT IT BACK! Batteries, birthday candles, lightbulbs, tools . . . NOTHING wastes precious time more than having to look around for crap.

A single MILF keeps a basket for shoes by the door. A single MILF needs all the help she can get, and this help comes in the form of a basket you can rely on to do one job and do it well. Catch shoes. Put such a container by your door so the kids can put their dirty shoes in it whenever they walk in. This way, you're not tripping all over shoes every time you walk around your house. (I have actually been taken out by a pile of shoes at the bottom of a staircase.) AND, most important, no more "MAAAAAaaa . . . I can't find my shoes!"

My second favorite household chore is ironing. My first being hitting my head on the top bunk bed until I faint.

—ERMA BOMBECK

A single MILF relies on takeout. Running kids from activity to activity, then having to go home, do homework and get dinner ready without the help of another grown-up is hard, if not almost impossible. There's nothing wrong with getting food to go. No one's going to judge you for not cooking a Martha Stewart–quality meal. Well, Martha may judge you, but I won't.

A single MILF has SUPER easy dinner tricks, including brinner. Breakfast + Dinner = Brinner. Kids love the idea of scrambled eggs and toast for dinner. It's good for them and SOOOOO easy! Single MILFs are also a fan of **make your own pizza night**, where the kids throw canned tomato sauce and mozzarella cheese on top of pita bread, and **make your own tacos night**, where you place shredded rotisserie chicken (EVERY market on the planet has these now), shredded Mexican cheese and sliced avocado in a tortilla. As with the pizza, the kids have fun cooking for themselves!

A single MILF forms a dinner circle with a couple of friends. One day a week, one mom can cook a meal big enough for all of the families in the circle (For sanity's sake, don't do more than two or three families total) and deliver it to them. Then two or three times a week you get meals from them. One day of work = two or three days of ease. WOO-HOO! MILFs like easy!

A single MILF isn't afraid to have a BAD Mommy Night! This is my absolute favorite tip from a MILFy friend that has saved me quite a few times (once when I was recovering from pneumonia). On that rare night that occurs maybe a couple of times a year where you are sick, have a headache or just feel like your ass is nailed to the floor—a night when you can't face making dinner, you don't care if your kids bathe and all you want is to be wheeled around in your bed like the Monkees in their opening TV show sequence ("Hey, hey!

We're the Monkees! . . .")—tell the kids it's "Bad Mommy Night" and let them have cereal for dinner. They can even bring it into your room to have a picnic on your bedroom floor. Let them make ice cream sundaes and just lie around your bed watching movies with you. Don't bathe. Don't brush teeth. Ignore hygiene altogether. And it's not the end of the world that they go one or two nights a year without a good cleansing or a square meal. You can always brush teeth in the morning, after the "meds" have kicked in. Embrace Bad Mommy Night—you'll be glad you did.

I know how to do anything—I'm a mom.

—ROSEANNE BARR

The Social Life of the Single MILF (Yes, She Can Have One!)

We've already established that a single MILF is definitely NOT a cougar. As such, I don't think it's necessary to discuss why it's not okay to drop your kids off at school in the leopard-striped dress you wore to a club the night before. Or why your children shouldn't have to say a polite good-bye to the strange man coming out of your bedroom. These things just wouldn't happen. Not to a MILF.

But of course a single MILF does date and understands that the care and feeding of her inner woman is as important as her well-being as a mother. Besides, dating is one of the perks of being single! There are, though, some strategies that have worked for other single MILFs that have allowed them to enjoy guilt-free dating and still feel like responsible moms.

"Continuity, continuity, continuity!" says Betsy Brown Braun, parenting guru and author of *Just Tell Me What to Say* and *You're Not the Boss of Me*. Stick to routines and try to keep life as predictable as you possibly can for your children. Continuity is the key to helping your kids cope with any changes and balancing your need for a little "me" time. With that in mind:

A single MILF picks a night once a week and makes it her regular "night out." Schedule dates, classes and/or outings with girlfriends on that night every week. That way, when the night comes around, the kids expect it to be your evening out. There is a lot less whining when kids know what to expect. And you'll wake up looking forward to the same day every week for that reason.

A single MILF uses a regular babysitter. This way, your kids know when to expect you are going out and know what to expect from their evening. Having the same babysitter week after week allows them to build a comfort zone with someone else and find a way to feel safe and content while you're out.

A single MILF plans her kids' dinners with them for the nights she's out. Let them pick what they like so they have something to look forward to on those evenings. Chicken nuggets or macaroni and cheese? Just knowing they get a treat when you go out helps soothe the restless natives.

A single MILF does not introduce dates to her kids. Meet outside your home, at a coffeehouse, a restaurant, or a movie theater. It's hard for kids, especially ones who have gone through a divorce, to see their mother with different men. They just have no way of understanding what dating is all about, and if the guy turns out to be a loser, they'll never see him again. It's all too confusing. Keep the kids out of your dating life.

I'm not even going to *touch* on making recommendations about when the appropriate time is to introduce your kids to someone you're dating. I've heard stories of moms who won't introduce a man till they know they're getting remarried and stories of moms who wait only a few months into the relationship. There are still others who don't want to deal with the issue at all and swear they won't date till their youngest turns eighteen. (You can identify these women by their constant verbal affirmation that they don't need sex, and their incredibly time-consuming/detail-intensive hobbies. You can't possibly think about sex when you're re-creating the Statue of Liberty out of toothpicks.) Everyone needs to do what works for her.

As for me? My kids met my boyfriend after six months. However, he didn't sleep over until a year and a half later. (At least, they didn't know he was sleeping over. . . . A knock on my locked bedroom door sounded the alarm of incoming children. We'd hear a knock and he'd go hide in my closet. Yes . . . this worked and they never knew . . . until now . . . because my kids are probably reading this . . . um . . . Hi, kids! Mommy loves you. . . .)

"Mommy? Who's that man in your bed?"

So you've just been woken up in the middle of the night by a tugging on your covers. You open your eyes and find yourself face-to-face with a wide-eyed five-year-old who is simultaneously clinging to her blanket and pointing at the "strange" man next to you. Of course, you've been dating the guy for six months, but your daughter has no idea who he is—she's never seen him. What do you do? Wake him up and lie. Lie like your life depended on it. Introduce them in a very matter-of-fact style. "Honey, this is my friend Tim." (If he offers a handshake, that's a nice touch, but if turning over will reveal nakedness, a friendly wave from the far side of the bed will do.) "He's a really good friend and he couldn't get his car to work so I said he could sleep over." Then dangle a sparkly object in front of her and hope she forgets the whole thing.

But whatever you do, don't let your child see that you're naked.

"Mommy? Who's that man in your bed . . . and why are you naked?"

Uh, find a good child therapist.

> By and large, mothers and housewives
> are the only workers who do not
> have regular time off. They are
> the great vacationless class.
>
> —ANNE MORROW LINDBERGH

Obviously, in addition to the daily challenges of mother-hood, the single MILF is faced with her own unique set of challenges—and she handles them all with tremendous aplomb. With all of the challenges the single MILF tackles alone on a daily basis, this amazing, agile and wholly "complete" mom deserves the honor of being labeled a MILF.

Working mothers are guinea pigs in a scientific experiment to show that sleep is not necessary to human life.

—AUTHOR UNKNOWN

the
"MILF's MILF"

THE MILF AND FRIENDSHIP

> Friendship is born at that moment when one person says to another, "What! You too? I thought I was the only one."
>
> —C. S. LEWIS

They say that "behind every great man is a great woman." Well, behind every great woman are her MILFs. (To say "great" MILFs would just be redundant.) These strong, intelligent, supportive girlfriends know everything about you (i.e. your favorite dessert is chocolate pudding; you're afraid of birds; you wear only thong underwear; you weigh yourself before and after you pee just to see how much weight you've lost . . .) and they love you anyway. They're upbeat, stylish, and they've got it all together—or at least admit to it when they don't.

These MILFs are known as . . . well . . . MILFs. But in *this* case, the acronym stands for "Mother I'd Like to Be *Friends* With." (This is where you say, "Aaaahhhhh, very clever" . . . or not.) It is a well-known fact that MILFs make the best friends. They're smart, they're interesting and they're fun at cocktail parties. Like a well-made martini, they're smooth, classy and intoxicating. You can't help but want to be near them.

These fabulous MILFs keep us strong and help us feel like we're not insane (unless we really are—then they smuggle brownies into the asylum for us). They're an integral part of our roles as women, mothers and wives, as they grip our hands tightly to help stop us from slipping into the quicksand of our lives. A MILF knows the value of her friends and cherishes them.

Most important, these MILFs are caring, loyal and not afraid of your children (unless they should be . . .). They bring us dinner when we're sick, pick up our mail when we're on vacation and take our children for sleepovers when we desperately need a date night but can't get a babysitter. A MILF will always tell you if you look fat in those jeans, need to color your hair, or that it's seriously time to wax. They clap for us when we succeed, dust us off when we fail and continue to encourage us to try new things.

MILF friends are a part of us. Whether they're a mom we see on the school yard every day, a college roommate we talk to only every few months, or the best friend from childhood who stood up for us in sixth grade when Tommy McSomething-or-other said we had cooties. Friends are a part of us—they shape us, mold us and are the most sincere reflection of ourselves.

If it weren't for our MILFs, we'd just be wives, moms and colleagues. Of course, that's fine, and admirable—but it's not very MILFy. Why? Because being a wife/mom/colleague is only part of being a MILF. These roles are only a fraction of who we are. A MILF would no more want to be seen solely as a mother or wife than she would want to be seen solely as a president, vice president or executive grand poo-bah. A MILF is so much more! Sure, we can look to our careers for fulfillment, our husbands and boyfriends for love, and our children to bring meaning to our lives. But a MILF needs her fellow MILFs. They nurture her spirit and fuel "the woman inside": the woman who loves to travel, who enjoys wine, who cooks, who laughs at fart jokes, who loves a good romance novel, who dabbles in photography, who speaks ten different languages—and who is screaming, "Get me the hell OUT of here! I'm going insane!" in each and every one of them.

A Friend for All Seasons

Friends are the reflection of the many different facets of our personalities—and if there's one thing MILFs have . . . it's facets. Life is complicated, motherhood is complicated, and we, as MILFs, are complicated and often contradictory: we need friends who love yoga and friends who hate working out; friends for whom motherhood is a breeze and friends who get completely overwhelmed; friends who love to laugh and friends who love a good cry. For one friend to be all of these things, she would have to be schizophrenic. (However, the fact that *you* are all these things does not make you schizophrenic—it simply makes you "mercurial.") The point is, no one person can be everything, and that's okay.

For a MILF, friendship means having a variety of friends. (Notice I don't say *lots* of friends—having a ton of friends does not make you a MILF; it just makes you unavailable.) Different friends enhance different parts of our lives—you may have a friend who loves concerts and current events, another friend who loves to go out and hit new restaurants, and then a friend who's perfect to call upon for casual potluck family dinners. What is important to remember is that you don't have to find all of these characteristics in one person.

I'm not saying you should spread yourself thin. Between kids, a spouse, school and work, aren't you thin enough? You're the Twiggy of motherhood. No one can be a good friend to that many people. It's not physically possible. But cultivating some good friendships, strong friendships, friendships that feed your soul, with a variety of different people simultaneously makes you feel grounded and helps broaden your horizons. (MILFs like broad horizons.)

It's just very rarely that we come across that one "perfect" person who gets check marks in all categories across the chart. The truth is, throughout your life you'll meet many MILFs—at preschool, on the soccer field, at work, through friends. Some will stay forever, and some will fade away, but that doesn't make them any less important.

Curdled MILF: When Friendship Expires . . .

Sex and the City is a movie. Well, it was a book first and then a TV show and then it was a movie.

It's important to point this out because a substantial number of women believe you should have one group of women with whom you do everything, go everywhere and confide all, and if you don't, you are "missing out." I know. . . . I was one of them.

For years, I had a group of friends with whom I did everything. We organized big group playdates, went to dinner together and left soup on one another's doorsteps when one of us was sick. One of these women was my best friend. Our kids were best friends. Our husbands were best friends. It was perfect—for eight years—then it wasn't. What happened? I don't know. I wonder if anyone ever really knows why their friendships fall apart. Whenever you hear a story about a lost friendship, that person always seems to say, "I have no idea what happened." You have your side of the story, the other person has theirs, and somewhere in the middle is the reason why it all went to pot.

I have since learned that as we get older and have families, the job description of "friend" changes. In elementary school, it's "Play with me." In high school, it's "Be here for me—always!" In college, it's "Be here for me—unless I have a guy in the room—or am in Spain for the semester. . . ." And now, as a mom with a family of my own, it's "If you can be here for me when I really need you, that's good enough for me." I don't look to one friend—or even one group of friends—for happiness. Not anymore. I have a wide variety of friends with whom I can indulge in the wide variety of things I like to do and be. My family and my boyfriend provide me with love and encouragement and it leaves me available to enjoy the friends I have for what they're able to offer me with their busy lives. Fun, laughter, love and, when I really need it, a bowl of soup on my doorstep.

MILF Mantra: To have a friend, be a friend.

The MILF's MILF Rule

A MILF understands the importance of friendship and knows that in order to *have* go-to gals, you have to *be* a go-to gal. And it's not always easy—you're not in college anymore. It's much harder to stay close when you can't just roll out of bed in the morning and tell your BFFs about the guy who just left. You have families, jobs, hobbies, PTA, a crappy housekeeper . . . you know . . . *life*! But a MILF understands the role her fellow MILFs play in her life and she doesn't take them for granted.

If a MILF makes plans with friends, she does her best to keep them. Even when she's feeling lazy or tired, she will MILF up! (I just came up with that. . . .) It means a MILF will **get** her act together and **go** meet her friend. Because MILFs don't cancel at the last minute for any reason other than fever (theirs or their child's), blood (theirs or their child's) or a natural disaster. It's selfish. And MILFs know they don't have to look perfect to be fabulous, so they can rely on their shortcuts to "turn it out" with minimum energy. Maybe she'll take a quick shower, slick her hair back into a chic bun and pull out one of her "pre-organized" outfits for just such an emergency. Or, at the very least, she'll slide on a little deodorant and put on a clean T-shirt. The point is, MILFs don't think about how tired they are when they have a commitment. They simply MILF up! (Okay . . . I'll stop using it now. . . .)

A MILF in Need Is a MILF Indeed

A MILF knows good friends are worth their weight in platinum, and making the people around her feel cherished is part of what makes her so MILFy.

A MILF pinch-hits. When a friend is sick or in her "fourth" trimester, a MILF shows up with dinner, or a great movie, or maybe just her minivan to pick up her friend's children and watch them for a couple hours so her friend can rest.

A MILF calls or texts her pal when a favorite store is having a sale or there's a great deal at the market.

A MILF lets her friend know when she runs into her ex and tells her how much better off she is without him.

A MILF sends flowers with a note, or even just an e-mail, when a friend is "down," just to let her know she's thinking of her.

A MILF organizes a girls' night out (even if it's every twelve months). If you have ever gone to a movie on a weeknight, headed to a spa for the weekend, or had dinner at a hot new restaurant, you've seen them: groups of MILFs talking, laughing and drinking together. They're dressed up, they're animated and they look delicious. Sometimes the only way to have a conversation is to get out of the house without the kids. Who can catch up on gossip when you have a bunch of kids constantly harassing you? A night out gives you time to catch up. It seems like bars everywhere have nights set aside for GNOs. Drink specials, nibblies, friends . . . perfecto.

great ideas for GNO

Follow hot restaurants in town and try new ones each time.

Want to keep it cheap? Have the girls over to your house and make dinner together. After the kids are in bed you can catch up. Have teenagers who stay up late? Send them to a friend's for a sleepover.

Karaoke—Girls love to sing. Even when we suck, we love to sing. We'll sing in groups; we'll sing solo; we'll sing lead; we'll sing backup. We'll sing anything, anytime, anywhere. (You should hear me in my car—my kids hate it!) Just keep some throat lozenges handy.

Wine tastings—You can usually find a local restaurant hosting one of these events. It's a great activity for a night out with the girls and is surprisingly informative! (Did you know that cream of tartar is made from tartaric acid—the powder that builds up on the inside of a cask of aging wine? Now you do.)

Knitting club—or any hobby in which you all share an interest. Get together regularly to do it together.

A MILF keeps in touch. MILFs like to know what's going on with their girlfriends, but it's hard to find the time to talk on the phone. Join Twitter, Facebook, MySpace, Flickr—even share stories you read and like via Amplify. These social networks make it easy to stay in touch—especially when your friends live in different time zones. Keeping up your page on these sites is so easy and it's like having your own personal little newsletter. It's easier than you think and it's free! But most important, you can catch up with all of your friends when you finally have five minutes to spare—which could very likely be at midnight.

'Tis the privilege of friendship to talk nonsense, and have her nonsense respected.

— CHARLES LAMB

A MILF organizes group family time. Sometimes getting time away from family just isn't a reality. So gather everyone together, kids and all. It's a great way to bond with family and friends simultaneously.

TIPS FOR FAMILY TIME:

Look into hotel packages for families traveling together. Get a group rate.

Consider camping. Or, as I like to call it, "glamping." This is when you go to a camping-like place but you have your own bathroom and microwave. Cook dinner together in the fire pit, make s'mores, someone can bring a guitar. (Someone always seems to have a guitar. . . .)

Arrange a softball game/kickball game. Get a field at the local park and have one big game together.

Have small children and can't make a game or glamping happen? Use that minivan and pack up for a day at the beach.

Nobody's conscience ever kept him awake at night from having exaggerated the good qualities of his friends.

—AUTHOR UNKNOWN

Mommy Dating

What if you're without good MILF girlfriends? Finding new mommy friends is tough. There seem to be only four big windows in life when women have the chance to meet other women with whom they'll forge deep, lasting

toxic people, emotional vampires and other things that go bump in the night . . .

Part of what makes a MILF such a good friend is her ability to weed out toxic people so she can focus on the important people in her life. Toxic people are those who work their way into your life only to turn everything to crap. They try to destroy your other friendships so that they can move "into position." They have no respect for your time, life revolves around them and they constantly ask for favors but never give anything in return. Quite frankly, when you think about it, you have no idea why you're friends, because they contribute nothing to your life. How do you know if someone is toxic? If whenever you spend time with a person, you feel like you've been pissed on, they are toxic. Want to feel fantastic again? Cut the cord and wave bye-bye.

The other "bad seed" is known as an "emotional vampire." They seek out happy people and try to drain them of their confidence. Their reason for this? When you start to doubt yourself, or feel low, they feel better about themselves. They trash your partner so they feel better about their own relationships and they go out of their way to make you feel just plain miserable. In fact, the more miserable you are, the happier they are. They feed off of your pain. They like to cause it and they like to fuel it. They make you feel badly about yourself, knock you down and hold you there only to build themselves up. They thrive off of your misery and just plain suck . . . literally.

friendships—elementary school, college, job, and when their kids go to preschool. Outside of those windows of opportunity, it's like finding the door to your crawl space. Finding like-minded MILFs to befriend outside of these venues is challenging, but it's not impossible. Mostly it just takes putting on a smile and being your outgoing, MILFy self.

Take a class. Take an evening class in something that interests you: photography, pottery, writing, scuba diving, Italian lessons, anything really. This will automatically put you with other people who share the same interests while broadening your own horizons.

Volunteer at your kids' school. Once your kids are in elementary school or older, there just aren't as many opportunities for parents to meet one another. Volunteering will not only keep you involved with your kids' school lives, but it is a great way to meet other moms who live in your neighborhood and have kids the same age.

Capitalize on your kids' activities. Do you talk to other moms while you wait for your kids or do you bring a book and close yourself off? Do you do the drop and dash? Stick around and be friendly.

Join a book club. Ask around or see if your local mom-and-pop bookstore knows of any.

Check out local museums. They usually have special events for families either on Sundays or in the evenings. It's a great way to meet like-minded people.

Google. Google "(*your town*) Groups" and see what comes up. Maybe it's a local museum group; maybe it's a group for parents of multiples. (If you have twins, the National Organization of Mothers of Twins Clubs has a chapter in almost every city.) Some cities have organized social groups, supper clubs and ways for couples to meet other parents—usually run by some parent organization. Another way to meet other parents in your city? Almost every city has at least one online parenting group (either via Yahoo or another engine) where you can get advice from other moms and share information.

Warning: Follow the group online for a while before you try this—so you can weed out the crazies (an unfortunate part of every online group). You'll discover that personalities emerge and maybe you'll find someone you'll click with (no pun intended) and can meet for coffee.

Motherhood: The Game

Motherhood does funny things to you. And by "funny," I don't mean the line down your belly you got when you were pregnant. I mean parenthood (that's fatherhood too, so stop laughing, DILFs!) makes some people do crazy things. And more than a few of these people will be friends—good friends—who used to seem so normal. You'd think parenting was an Olympic sport and they're the "home team." You, however, are now Russia.

When it comes to motherhood, the competition can really heat up and some women just feel the urge to "take out the opposition." Rest assured these women are not MILFs. But inevitably, if you're in Mommy & Me, out on a school yard or trying to get your teen through the college application process, you will be drawn into these games. Someone is going to want you on their team, backing her, confirming that she is indeed **the** #1 Mom! And as the battle lines against other moms are drawn, and the lines of friendship get crossed, it's important to remember one thing—if you get to the finish line first, that probably means you're dead. Now, does that sound like winning to you?

So here's a bit of advice for handling some of those "situations." (LEGAL NOTE: I cannot take any responsibility for the dirty looks, the *tsk tsk*s or the doors being slammed in your face that these responses provoke.)

Q: My friends are all trying to one-up each other—be the better mom, take the cooler classes, throw the better birthday party. . . . What do I do when I really don't want to go to "this" gym, take "that" class or throw huge parties for my kids? Signed, Not Interested in the Joneses

A: Dear "Not Interested,"

Why our "friends" approach parenting as some kind of competition is beyond me. I happen to know for a fact that no one has ever been rejected by Harvard because they didn't have David Beckham as a soccer coach or couldn't swim by six months. Let me ease your mind—your child does not need to speak fluent Japanese to succeed in life. Gymboree, soccer camp for eighteen-month-olds . . . SAT prep classes for kindergartners . . . all of these are OPTIONAL organized activities designed to entertain and stimulate the children of moms who don't know what else to do with their kids (*no* judgment here . . . I'm one of them!). If you are self-motivated, there are LOTS of things you can do that are just as good! Go to the park, build sand castles on the beach, take a nature walk around the block and hunt for snails. All of these activities will give your child the same stimulation as any organized activity—for a LOT less money. Want more social interaction for your child? Join a local playgroup—e-mail women in your neighborhood with children the same age and set something up at a local park. Chances are they're looking for other down-to-earth moms who don't want to pay David Beckham to teach their child soccer either. What a great way to meet other like-minded MILFs.

Ah, yes. And then there is the "birthday" thing. The odd belief that a child will somehow be *more* "seven" because he had a carousel, flamethrowers and a snake charmer to help usher in his birthday, while yours had only a peanut hunt and homemade cake. The reality is they're still both seven.

The truth is, some moms just need to feel superior, and the only way to do this is by worming around in other people's business and trying to make *you* feel inferior. Let me assure you—these women are not MILFs. If you can only feel good about yourself as a parent because you go on expensive vacations, take the "hottest" Mommy & Me classes and go to the most exclusive schools, you are a MILF Dud—an imposter of MILFiness. You can't be hot when you're only worth what you spend. We all want our children to have wonderful lives and great opportunities, but it's just not always physically, financially or logistically possible to take them on pony rides through the Andes over spring break. A MILF loves her children and is confident in her skills as a mother. And if you are friends with MILFs, they support you 110 percent. No contest. Why? A MILF has nothing to prove. But you can't stop the bragging and boasting of some parents, so here are a few suggested responses to those statements you'll no doubt hear from your so-called "friends":

Q: **My child is 90th percentile in height. The doctor says he's just growing like a weed! How big is your child?**

A: My child is 1/1073rd percentile. In fact, my child is so small he sleeps in a vacuum cleaner.

Q: **Between taking Boucle and Almond to all their activities—swim team, French horn lessons, jujitsu and Mandarin classes—I'm totally exhausted! But what's a mom to do? Colleges are so competitive these days— we want to have an edge. What does Olivia do?**

A: Livi? She sits on her ass. In fact, we thought we would invite little Boucle to come over next Thursday and sit on her ass with us. Would she like that?

Q: We're having Anthea's fifth birthday party at the Metropolitan Opera. They're going to wear the real costumes and put on their own opera . . . all in Italian! What are you doing for Scottie's birthday?

A: Wow! For Scottie's fifth birthday we're going to have Jorge the mechanic come and fix the car. The kids will hand him tools and use the jack—we're excited.

Friendships can be fabulous, and they can also get complicated. Just remember, *you* are a MILF! And your MILF girlfriends can't be beat! Know yourself, be confident with your choices as a mother and don't worry about what everyone else is doing. Or . . . you could just get some new friends.

(CHAPTER THIRTEEN)

spilled
MILF

WHEN A MILF GETS KNOCKED OVER

We no longer want to hit that. Get off MILF Island.

—HOST ON *30 ROCK*'S MOCK REALITY TV SHOW *MILF ISLAND,* TO A DUMPED CONTESTANT

Being a MILF isn't always great. And it's certainly not always easy. Especially when bad things happen or you are faced with a painful reality.

For example, my ex-husband's girlfriend is prettier than I am. Prettier, thinner and younger looking. How do I know this? My daughter told me. To my face—as I stood at my kitchen stove braising a pot of short ribs in bacon. It gets better. His girlfriend was standing there too—watching me make said short ribs—when my daughter blurted it out.

We were both horrified. I couldn't believe my daughter would say something so hurtful. Of course, she's ten. But it was clear . . . I was going to have to put her up for adoption.

I didn't know my ex's girlfriend was coming over. I certainly had no reason to expect her. My ex was supposed to pick up my son for some "private time," and when he showed up at my house, voilà, there she was. Right by his side. When I opened the door I was wearing my Sunday best—a twenty-year-old sweatshirt from my college alma mater, blue sweatpants and fuzzy slippers. My hair was dirty and piled into a bun on top of my head. My sweatshirt was covered in old grease stains I'd earned by cooking in it every Sunday for the past ten years (Yes . . . I wash it weekly) and the smell of bacon and short ribs permeating the house only reinforced the whole "I've obviously completely given up" *thing* I had going on.

It was humiliating. It certainly wasn't my MILFiest moment.

I didn't punish my daughter. Speaking her mind isn't a crime even when it's not what I want to hear. Besides, she has Asperger's syndrome, a form of autism, and calling things as she sees them is just a part of the package. She wasn't trying to hurt me. But hearing *her* truth killed me.

I didn't want my ex back, or the marriage. I have a boyfriend and we've been together for more than three years. I'm quite content. But divorce hurts—no matter who instigated it or how long ago you moved on—and when your former spouse moves on too and is happy, you can't help but wonder why *they* work when you guys couldn't. Your ex-spouse's newfound joy is some sort of proof that you are the problem. It can be completely disheartening.

That night, after my ex and his "thin, young, pretty" girl-friend left, I went through my nightly routine with the kids like nothing had happened. We ate the short ribs, took baths, brushed teeth and read books, and I kissed them all good night. Then I got into bed, still wearing my grease-stained sweatshirt, and cried. Boy, did I cry. The tears percolated up and out, uncontrollably, like an electric coffee urn that couldn't be unplugged. My boyfriend held me while the pain just poured out of me.

I cried because I knew I wasn't young anymore. I cried because I had a paunch where there used to be a flat stom-ach, and I cried because the man I had married, and with whom I'd had three children, had moved on. My marriage was officially over, and he was now with someone my kids thought was "better"—this woman whom my daughter barely knew, who had never been pregnant and fat and bloated, who had never given birth and who had never had to put her own wants and needs aside to care for a child (or two, or three . . .)—and it hurt like a m*therf@#ker! Suddenly, I felt ugly, old and "used."

This MILF had spilled all over the floor. And believe me, I was crying over it.

It happens to the best of us. And it doesn't have to be because we had some core-shaking revelation. Maybe your boss is an asshole that day (or for a week . . . or always), or you hate your new haircut, or your dog crapped all over the house and you had to spend the morning cleaning it up. Or perhaps you're just minding your own business, standing in line at Starbucks waiting for your daily vanilla latte, when your six-year-old son pokes you in the stomach, right where a bit of naked pudge has escaped from over your jeans and under your T-shirt, and says "Mommy, your stuffing is coming out" right in front of all of the people there—two of whom you know from the gym you haven't been to in months. . . . (This is hypothetical of course. . . .)

Maybe you feel bad because your husband isn't in the mood for sex. Few things can make a woman feel worse than offering it up on a 300-thread-count Egyptian cotton plate only to have the man you love hold up a hand and say, "Uh . . . pass." You know he's exhausted, or sick, or mourning the loss of his mother, but you're still, like, "Hey! I'm offering you SEX here!" Being turned down for sex just makes you feel so darn unMILFy.

My point is, whether you're married, divorced, single, whatever . . . there are times when you just don't feel like a MILF. The truth is, the world is filled with rejection—but you don't have to let it make you feel like a reject. YOU ARE A MILF! And you can clean it up and be as fresh as ever.

MILF Mantra: This too shall pass.

You don't have to hide from your pain in a pint of Ben & Jerry's, you don't have to get plastic surgery and you don't have to go on a major shopping spree to feel MILFy again. . . . (Okay . . . I bought some new shoes after that experience, but BOY do they make me feel "purdy"!)

The key is to NOT let it ruin your life. Okay, maybe you need a few days . . . and a hot fudge sundae. But a MILF doesn't let life get her down. Not for long. There are lots of things you can do to improve your mood. Simple things. It's not easy to motivate, but with a little internal kick in the pants, you too can remember that you're smart, vibrant and a great piece of ass.

Cleaning Up Spilled MILF

A MILF gets up, gets dressed and gets out! Want to feed a depression? Hang around the house in the same pajamas for days on end. Want to get over it and get on with your life? Get up out of bed, put on some clothes—something you feel good wearing—and get yourself out of the house! I don't care if you go to the market or just walk around the block. The point is, getting yourself out of the house and feeling good about how you look while you're there will improve your mood, get you back into the world and give you a jump-start toward helping you feel good again.

A MILF looks up. Literally. Stop looking at the ground. Nothing says "I'm not worthy, I'm not worthy, I'm not worthy . . ." like someone staring at the ground. Pick up your chin, look the world in the eye and act like you belong. *Flattering Perk*: your chin always looks better when it's lifted.

A MILF indulges in a pedicure and shows it off in strappy shoes. "Beauty is as beauty does. . . ." (All right, that wasn't quite the quote, but it works here. . . .) Get your toes done. Get a manicure. Making your body parts pretty and showing them off is a great way to lift your spirits.

A MILF pampers herself. Can't afford a day at the spa? Get a reflexology foot massage, or maybe even one of those chair massages they do at the mall. Who cares if someone you know sees you? If you can't be good to yourself, how can you expect anyone else to be good to you? Happy women make the best moms!

A MILF takes control. When you take control of your own choices, you'll feel stronger. You empower yourself. For example, cleaning up your space and putting it in order. Take all the crap off your kitchen table, put it on the floor and put it away. Take a bag and go around to everything that you can't stand looking at and put it away for a while. By the time you open it again, you know almost everything in it is outdated and you can get rid of most of it. But in the meantime, you'll have a space that makes you feel good. You can't feel good when you're surrounded by crap. MILFs don't like crap.

A MILF will eat smart food. A MILF doesn't keep a ton of crap in her pantry (maybe with the exception of those Pop-Tarts I discussed earlier, and an emergency bag of Oreos). This is so neither she nor the kids will fall victim to the "I'm bored" or "I'm sad" munchies. Keep healthy choices available (see the list of MILFy snack food). First thing in the morning, take out yogurt and pumpkin and cinnamon and put it in the fridge. Then food is ready for you. Take a

---

a few MILFy snack food ideas:

Sliced Red Peppers with Hummus

Honey Wheat Pretzels with Natural Peanut Butter

Whole Wheat Pita with Lite Cream Cheese

Apples and Peanut Butter (I lived on this through both of my pregnancies and now my kids love it too—go figure.)

Granola and Yogurt

snack bar with you for the afternoon. Bring gum with you at all times.

A MILF avoids toxic people. Hanging around these people—and you know who they are now—will only make you feel worse. And if they know you're down, they may even come looking for you. Screen their calls, don't make plans with them, and if they're unavoidable (which sometimes they are), don't get caught up in their false concern or weighed down in their sh*t when they decide to "share." They're out for themselves, and if you want to get out of your funk and feel good about yourself again, avoid them like the plague.

A MILF focuses on family. When you're sad or blue, go back to your "core"—the people you really love and who love you right back. Spend time nurturing and relishing the relationships of friends and family who care about you and will love you no matter what.

A MILF focuses on what's important. It's so easy to get stuck on the little things. And if the "things" aren't so little, it's even easier to cling to them. Try to think about your goals and move toward them. Remember what keeps you going. A MILF I know who is a life coach suggests a "vision board." Cut out images or words, or find symbols of things that make you happy or that you want. Arrange them together on a board or put them in a special journal where you can see what matters most and remember your goals every day.

A MILF cuts back on the gossip. Trashing other people when you feel crappy yourself may seem like a good way to feel better. After all, misery loves company. But ultimately, gossiping about other people just makes you feel crappier. It puts your head in a negative space, can create major guilt and could potentially create fallout you'll need to deal with later . . . like hurting someone's feelings, losing a friend or destroying a relationship. You know what? While you're at it, try to cut out the gossip altogether. (I'll try it with you. . . .)

A MILF exercises. MILFs know exercise is vital to their mental and physical health, but it's so very easy to feel overwhelmed by a busy schedule. So create a shortcut like one MILF I know: keep clean workout stuff in a bag by the door. And get out of the house early, before your day typically starts and before anyone is up. If you exercise on a stationary bike or treadmill, then bring a pad of paper so you can take notes of things you need to do and want to do throughout the day/ week. There aren't many moments when your head is clear, but this is one of them. Use it! I personally prefer burst-like interval training. I call it "brain scrubbing." I walk as quickly as I can for forty-five minutes to an hour. Every five minutes or so I inject increasingly longer sprints or lunges. I start with a sprint for thirty seconds and work my way up to bursts of extreme activity that last one minute. When I'm done I feel like my brain is cleaner. (NOTE: This exercise plan has not been endorsed by any doctor, trainer or even a really fit person. It just works for me. You should always consult with your doctor before starting any exercise routine and figure out a plan that works for you.)

A MILF calls her girlfriend. Girls need their friends. Hanging out with girlfriends and enjoying a cocktail is a time-honored tradition (or at least it should be). Don't drink? Meet for coffee. Go for a walk. Arrange a "family dinner" and have a girlfriend bring her kids—make dinner together. Being with someone who loves you and cares about your well-being is perhaps one of the best ways to get yourself out of a funk.

A MILF gives herself a little downtime. All of the above being said, acting like you're not upset is a great way to power through for the short term. But pretending a problem doesn't exist won't help you put it behind you. You can only shelve a bad feeling for so long. Give yourself a little time to examine a problem. Figure it out. Maybe just have a good cry. Get a therapist if you need one. I'm not saying you should wallow. I am saying you should allow yourself to feel badly sometimes. Life can suck. We all know it. But learning and growing from your experiences is what's going to add to your MILFiness. You can't grow if you always pretend everything is status quo.

A woman can say more in a sigh
than a man can say in a sermon.

—ARNOLD HAULTAIN

A MILF fakes it till she makes it. None of the above work for you? You've tried facials, cocktails, therapy, diets, meditation, crying, voodoo? Still feel like crap? Studies show that putting a smile on your face and going through the motions as if you were happy could eventually help you to feel better. Again, I'm not saying you should pretend everything is fine. But you can, and you should: Get Up! Get Dressed! And GET OUT! Along those lines . . .

A MILF knows that Xanax is not a four-letter word. Neither is Zoloft, Prozac or Lexapro. Don't be embarrassed to medicate if you think you need it. (Of course . . . you should talk to your doctor first.)

A MILF goes green. Researchers from the University of Essex in England discovered that just five minutes of a "green activity" like going for a walk, biking, gardening—anything that gets you interacting with the great outdoors—can lift your mood and your self-esteem.

Once you're knocked over, it can feel like you'll never pull it together again. But Spilled MILF isn't permanent. Remember, that which does not kill you . . . makes a great story.

CHAPTER FOURTEEN

25 rules for obtaining and maintaining maximum f@#kability

1. Own it! Doubt is for twenty-year-olds.

2. Wear sexy lingerie, even if no one is going to see it.

3. Laugh. A lot!

4. Wear shoes that fit. No one is sexy when her face is twisted in pain.

5. Exercise. It gives you the strength and energy you need to run after kids, and the endorphins make you feel GREAT!

6. Don't take shit.

7. Squeeze your kids in public till they tell you you're embarrassing them.

8. Kiss your husband/boyfriend in public.

9. Explore your sexuality and indulge it.

10. Eat like you enjoy it.

11. Wear sunscreen.

12. Don't try to be twenty again. You're not. And thank God!

13. Turn up the music while you make dinner and dance around the kitchen.

14. Wax.

15. Make a new friend. Getting to know fresh and interesting people keeps you fresh and interesting.

16. Look up! It fights gravity and you might see something new.

17. Shower every day.

18. Never carry a diaper bag that has bunnies or bears on it.

19. Be passionate about one thing other than your family.

20. NEVER EVER dress like your child!

21. Don't exercise wearing makeup unless your face looks good melting.

22. Sing like a rock star in the car.

23. Eat fruit, but don't call it dessert.

24. Don't be afraid to break out the bling. That diamond-and-sapphire ring you inherited from your grandmother, those diamond studs you never wear—feel free to saddle up! You've earned it and you can finally get away with it!

25. Don't listen to lists like this because you've lived long enough to know better.

final thought

THE POWER OF MILF

With great f@#kability comes great responsibility . . .

—AN ANONYMOUS MILF

This morning, before I sat down to write about "the power of MILF," I took a shower, put on a nice clean orange T-shirt (I look good in orange) and brushed on a little mascara.

My mission: channel my own inner MILF.

I wanted to *feel* like I had "the power of MILF" so I could really *speak* to those of you ready to harness your MILFy power—to really *prepare* you . . . but I was still very sleepy. (My son woke me up at two thirty in the morning because of a bad dream. Then his twin sister woke me up five minutes later to tell me she was going to go pee, in case I was interested. I wasn't.) But I had a job to do and no one was going to stop and wait for me to get fifteen minutes' more sleep, or for my coffee to kick in, or for me to just plain "get a grip"—so I did what any self-respecting MILF would do. I got up, I got dressed and I got out!

And you know what? I feel pretty darn good because of it.

A lot has changed since that day my friend called me a MILF: I have moved on from a failed marriage and found happiness with a great man and my life; I have made a new home for me and my three children, and can now drive past my old "dream house" (which is on the way to the park) without barfing; I've said farewell to some old friendships and made a few new ones; and I've moved past the horrible "falling-out" my youthful metabolism and I had when I turned forty, and have come to embrace the body that time, age and motherhood have bestowed upon me. But what pleases and surprises me the most when I look in the mirror is that I have kissed and waved good-bye to the young wife and mother who doubted her beliefs and her own value—and have come to embrace the complete woman I now see looking back at me. (And, might I say, she's pretty f@#king great.)

All of these things I've done because I believe and accept one simple premise: I am a MILF.

And you are too. You're the complete package: alluring, funny, confident, stylish, smart, savvy, kind, thoughtful, loving, giving, vibrant and sexy. And now *your* assignment is to go forth and share your fabulousness with everyone around you.

Well, I have spilled a little coffee on my T-shirt and the "perfection" I achieved this morning has worn off. But I am still writing, I'm still pursuing my passion and I feel really, really happy. Coffee-stained T-shirt and all.

Hey . . . a cute guy just walked into the coffee shop and smiled at me.

Yup. I am a MILF. Mission accomplished.

bibliography

The American Academy of Achievement, Washington, D.C., Coretta Scott King Biography: http://www.achievement.org/autodoc/page/kin1bio-1

Answers.com: WikiAnswers: "When was Bathsheba born?": http://wiki.answers.com/Q/When_was_Bathsheba_born

Bailly, Jenny, "Beauty Tips from *O, The Oprah Magazine* Beauty Editors": http://lifestyle.msn.com/your-look/makeup-skin-care-hair/staticslideshowoprah.aspx?cp-documentid=18634361

Bee, Peta, MailOnline (DailyMail.co.uk): "What Alcohol Really Does to Your Body": http://www.dailymail.co.uk/health/article-994/What-alcohol-really-does-body.html

Chu, Ying, "Facing the Big 3-0" by Ying Chu: http://www.marieclaire.com/hair-beauty/trends/articles/aging-skin-turning-30

Edmunds.com: "Top 10 Features Every Minivan Should Have," by editors at Edmunds.com: http://www.edmunds.com/reviews/list/top10/116141/article.html

Funny Mom Quotes: http://www.grinningplanet.com/funny-quotes/funny-mom-quotes.htm

Jameson, Noel, Funny Mom Quotes: http://www.momscape.com/articles/funny-mom-quotes.htm

Lipman, Marvin, MD, ConsumerReports.org: "Do You Drink Too
    Much? How To Tell": http://www.consumerreports.org/health/
    healthy-living/health-safety/do-you-drink-too-much/overview/
    do-you-drink-too-much.htm

Nellis, Cynthia, About.com Guide: Fashion Over 40 with Style Expert
    Kim Johnson Gross: http://fashion.about.com/od/stylebasics/a/
    fashionover40.htm

Quote Garden: Quotations for Mother's Day: http://www.quotegarden
    .com/mom-day.html

Renna, Christian, DO, LifeSpan Medicine, 2008: http://goop.com/
    newsletter/6/en/GwynethPaltrow

Ruud, Maddie, Touching and Funny Quotes about Mothers: http://
    hubpages.com/hub/quotes-about-mothers

Suite101: Single Mom Quotes—Motivational Aid for Single Mothers:
    http://parentingresources.suite101.com/article.cfm/single-mom-
    quotes—motivational-aid-for-single-mothers#ixzz0xNr0lF2c

Tanner, Lindsey, Associated Press, "Four Bad Habits Can Age You By
    12 Years: Common Sins of the Sedentary Make You Die Sooner
    and Seem Older": http://www.msnbc.msn.com/id/36786312/

What is Bamboo: http://www.wisegeek.com/what-is-bamboo-fabric.htm

Wikipedia.org: "Benazir Bhutto": http://en.wikipedia.org/wiki/Benazir_Bhutto

Wikipedia.org: "Jacqueline Kennedy": http://en.wikipedia.org/wiki/
    Jacqueline_Kennedy_Onassis

Wikipedia.org: "Nero": http://en.wikipedia.org/wiki/Nero

Wikipedia.org: "Queen Noor of Jordan": http://en.wikipedia.org/wiki/
    Queen_Noor_of_Jordan

Wikipedia.org: "Wang Zhaojun": http://en.wikipedia.org/wiki/Wang_Zhaojun

Yahoo.com: http://news.yahoo.com/s/ap/us_med_bad_habits_survival